Language

Knowledge for
Secondary Teachers

Also available:

Grammar Survival
A Teacher's Toolkit
Geoff Barton
1-84312-343-6

English Teaching in the Secondary School 2e
Linking Theory and Practice
Mike Fleming and David Stevens
1-84312-128-X

Grammar for Improving Writing and Reading
Geoff Dean
1-84312-003-8

Improving Learning in Secondary English
Geoff Dean
1-84312-146-8

Speaking, Listening and Drama
Andy Kempe and Jan Holroyd
1-84312-041-0

Language
Knowledge for
Secondary Teachers

Alison Ross

with Philippa Hunt

 David Fulton Publishers

Dedication
Dedicated to the memory of Ian MacKay Ross (1921–2005)

David Fulton Publishers Ltd
The Chiswick Centre, 414 Chiswick High Road, London W4 5TF

www.fultonpublishers.co.uk

David Fulton Publishers is a division of Granada Learning Limited, part of ITV plc

First published in Great Britain in 2006 by David Fulton Publishers

10 9 8 7 6 5 4 3 2 1

Note: The right of the individual contributors to be identified as the authors of their work has been asserted by them in accordance with the Copyright, Designs and Patents Act 1988.

Copyright © Alison Ross 2006

British Library Cataloguing in Publication Data
A catalogue record for this book is available from the British Library

ISBN 1 84312 358 4

Typeset by FiSH Books, Enfield, Middx.
Printed and bound in Great Britain

Contents

v

Acknowledgements

I would like to offer my sincere thanks to Philippa Hunt for her helpful criticism and support throughout the writing of the book. I would also like to thank the many friends, colleagues and students who have provided me with so many ideas over the years.

Alison Ross
November 2005

Grammar

Introduction

The aim of this book is to provide secondary English teachers with the knowledge about language required in the National Curriculum (DfEE/QCA, 2000) and the National Literacy Strategy Framework for Key Stages 3 and 4. It covers the essential concepts for language study, introducing the terminology needed for 'talking about language' and shows how this knowledge can be applied to the skills of reading, writing, speaking and listening.

The book is divided into two main sections:

- **Section 1** deals with grammar and the structure of language.
- **Section 2** moves outside the scope of sentence structure to explore aspects of:
  - phonology – the sounds of language and their effects
  - semantics – the ways words convey meanings via emotive and figurative language
  - discourse – the study of whole texts in context, including structure, genre, purpose, audience
  - pragmatics – the ways meanings are conveyed in social interaction.

The organisation of the book involved a common dilemma for teaching approaches: 'Where should I start?'

A 'top-down' approach emphasises the importance of the wider picture, before studying smaller elements. It may be more effective to begin study of a Shakespeare play by watching a performance of the whole text. But perhaps important aspects of context need to be appreciated before this: the conventions of the dramatic genre, or the historical and social background. Close analysis of speeches and individual words comes later.

The decision to take a 'bottom-up' approach to language study in this book was not taken lightly. Although a focus on words and sentences runs the risk of being de-contextualised, there are some practical advantages in working up from the basic elements of language. The educational background of the readers of this book also influenced the decision. Many university degrees in English emphasise the study of literature, rather than language. Although such courses involve the study of language in its wider aspects – genre, metaphor, rhetoric, and so on – finer details of grammar remain a source of uncertainty. This area, therefore, is tackled before the more familiar aspects.

The fact that the section on grammar is relatively long does not indicate that the *structure* of language is more important than other aspects of language in *use*, but rather that the grammatical terms and concepts are less familiar to readers under the age of 50. The reasons for this 'gap' in knowledge are connected with the changes in educational policy over the last few decades. These are worth exploring.

Knowing about language or using language?

Debates about English education tend to focus on the relative merits of explicit grammar study versus exposure to a rich variety of language use. The most notice-able changes have been in attitudes to the role of grammar. Using an analogy, I would suggest that trams are to transport policy as grammar is to educational policy; both have moved in and out of favour in recent history. In the 1950s there was a system of trams or trolley buses in most cities. They were considered an effi-cient form of public transport. Then they seemed outdated and the whole system was dismantled. Around the turn of the 21st century, the advantages of this mode of transport were recognised and tram systems were reintroduced. Some people complain about the expense and inconvenience. For others, trams have intrinsic value, but their role is important in the wider scheme of things: trams contribute to a more efficient and environmentally friendly transport system.

Changing attitudes to the role of grammar teaching have followed a similar path. From the eighteenth century until the 1960s, a formal approach to teaching the structures of language was accepted as the most effective way to teach English (and foreign) languages. By the 1970s, grammar study was seen as outdated and inefficient. These conclusions were based on research studies, showing that explicit teaching of grammar had little impact on the wider skills of language use (Wilkinson, 1971). It was replaced by a 'language in use' approach, where the emphasis was on exposure to various forms of language, without the need for the terminology to describe language. Later studies cast doubt on the validity of these conclusions (Tomlinson, 1994). After decades of teaching English without any explicit reference to grammar, the National Curriculum (1989, revised in 2000) caused another change in the ways English was taught in schools. The reinstate-ment of grammar – as with trams – has been welcomed by many with nostalgia for bygone days, when rules were fixed and order prevailed. However, this is not simply a return to the grammar teaching of the past. The contemporary, 'stream-lined' approach to grammar no longer emphasises the value of 'naming of parts' for its own sake. Grammar is now seen to have an unfulfilled potential for its contribu-tion to the wider scheme of things. As the linguist David Crystal comments:

> The principle was evident: one should not teach structures without showing children how these structures are used in real-life situations; and, conversely, one should not intro-duce children to the language of real-life situations without giving them some means of

talking about it precisely. Structure and use should be seen as two sides of the same coin – a view which is present in the guidelines which led to the new British National Curriculum course on English. But the question remained; how exactly can these two domains be brought together?

(Crystal, 1998)

We can see the two aspects of language *structure* and *use* combined in the National Curriculum policy for the overall aims of English education. There are three strands regarding the aims for language use, with attainment targets from Levels 1 to 8:

- **EN1:** speaking and listening
- **EN2:** reading
- **EN3:** writing.

The concept of language variation shapes the overall statement of aims for attainment. Pupils should become aware, not only of the conventions of standard English, but of the ways in which language varies according to the different types of use, by reading a variety of texts, writing for a range of purposes and adapting their speech for different contexts.

The requirements for language structure emphasise the importance of knowledge about the way language works: 'Pupils should be taught the principles of sentence grammar and whole-text cohesion and use this knowledge in their writing.'

Based on this statement of overall aims, more specific guidelines were developed in the National Literacy Strategy. The Framework for Teaching English provided a clear, extensive programme of explicit terms for describing the structure of language at Key Stages 1 and 2. This, in turn, created the need for a more rigorous literacy strategy at Key Stages 3 and 4. (NB: Key Stage 4 is still in outline at the time of writing).

The Framework indicates how this knowledge about language can be applied to pupils' use of language, using a division into three levels of language structure: Word, Sentence and Text (DfES, 2001).

- At *word level*, there are applications to spelling and vocabulary.
- At *sentence level*, applications to sentence construction, punctuation and awareness of standard English in the context of language variation and change.
- At *text level*, applications to skills of reading, writing, speaking and listening.

The organisation of the book follows this distinction between levels of language:

Section 1

morphology	word level
word class	word level
phrase	sentence level
clause	sentence level
sentence	sentence level

Section 2

phonology	word level
semantics	word level
discourse	text level
pragmatics	text and context

The teaching approaches used in the book aim to combine knowledge about language with skills in using language. Before outlining these, it is necessary to clarify the definition of 'grammar' – the subject of Section 1.

What is grammar?

When David Crystal was invited to provide a definition of grammar that could be understood by a bright child, he offered this: 'Grammar is the way we make sentences.' This is delightfully simple, but it is necessary to be aware of some differences in the way the term 'grammar' is used and understood. For a word that is mentioned so often in debates about education, its meaning is surprisingly elusive.

This is partly because of the emotive associations that the word has acquired. The title of 'grammar school' for those pupils who passed the 11-plus examination suggested that grammar was the preserve, and even the major concern, of the educational elite. Feelings about other school subjects – such as Maths, Science, History and Geography – are generally neutral. Knowing about grammar is often a source of pride, embarrassment or even resentment. For some people, the study of grammar is connected with order and discipline. The Conservative politician Norman Tebbit once suggested that there was a correlation between the loss of grammar and crime rates.

The distinction between prescriptive and descriptive approaches to grammar is worth noting. The first grammar books in the 18th century aimed to codify the rules of English language. The approach was **prescriptive**, assuming that there exists one 'correct' or 'proper' way of structuring sentences. The model used by these writers was the Latin language, and some of the rules they proposed are still accepted without question today. A frequently mentioned rule is that you should never split an infinitive. Fowler perceptively comments:

> The English-speaking world may be divided into (1) those who neither know nor care what a split infinitive is; (2) those who do not know, but care very much; (3) those who know and condemn; (4) those who know and approve; (5) those who know and distinguish. Those who neither know nor care are the vast majority, and are a happy folk, to be envied by most of the minority classes.
>
> (Fowler, 1965)

For those readers in group (2) – who do not know, but care very much – the infinitive is the base form of the verb, 'to go'. A famous example of a split infinitive occurs in the introduction to *Star Trek*: 'to boldly go where no man has gone before.' The reason for saying that infinitives should not be split is based on Latin, where infinitives are single words (*vincere* – 'to conquer'), so cannot be split. Many people challenge the assumption that what was true for Latin must also be true for English.

If a prescriptive approach functions rather like a guide to etiquette, a **descriptive** approach, as its name suggests, aims to describe the structures of language in more neutral terms. The National Literacy Strategy emphasises this disinterested reflection on contemporary uses of English. This involves awareness of language variation and change, in particular differences between speech and writing, formal and colloquial language, regional dialects and standard English. Although a descriptive approach acknowledges that language may vary according to its context, standard English is still 'prescribed' for public communication; for example, Level 4 and above must use standard English when appropriate. The prescriptive approach, though diluted, is still apparent in attitudes to prestige of standard forms of language.

There is also some confusion between the terms **syntax** and **grammar**. Although the terms are sometimes used interchangeably to refer to the structure of language, some make a slight distinction. The official website for the Department for Education and Science uses 'grammar' as the overall term, distinguishing between 'syntax' and 'morphology'.

> Grammar is the study of the way language is organised, especially the rules which are used between words (syntax) and within words (morphology).
>
> (http://www.standards.dfes.gov.uk)

So, grammar – including syntax and morphology – may be defined as 'the way language is organised' or 'the way we make sentences'. In *A Dictionary of Stylistics* (Wales, 2001), grammar is explained as 'the study of form'. Others refer to the 'structure of words or sentences'. The metaphor of building, or construction, is common to all. But what sort of construction is a sentence?

What type of structure?

On the page, sentences may look like a linear, **two-dimensional** structure. However, it is misleading to regard language as individual words, linked one after another in a string. For example, if we want to find out what occurs before a verb and look at the order of individual words in these sentences, there is no apparent pattern:

Teenagers	*upset me.*	*teenagers*	*(noun)*
They	*upset me.*	*they*	*(pronoun)*
Their refusal to move	*upset me.*	*move*	*(verb)*
Swearing loudly	*upsets me.*	*loudly*	*(adverb)*
Leaving lights on	*upsets me.*	*on*	*(preposition)*

A more helpful analogy is a **three-dimensional** structure, such as one created from Lego building blocks. Although the smallest unit is a single brick – or word – larger forms, such as walls or roofs, can operate as elements in the structure. In language, these larger elements are phrases and clauses. The three-dimensional structure of language can be summarised as a hierarchy of levels:

TABLE 1.1 Levels of structure

One or more **morphemes**	combine to form	words.
One or more **words**	combine to form	phrases.
One or more **phrases**	combine to form	clauses.
One or more **clauses**	combine to form	sentences.
One or more **sentences**	combine to form	paragraphs and whole texts.

Section 1 moves up through these levels to sentence structure, with exploration of text structure in Section 2 (Chapter 13 on discourse).

Another helpful analogy for the structure of language is the game, Jenga, building a tower from wooden blocks. The object is to add, remove or replace pieces without destroying the overall structure. This is similar to the construction of sentences: a basic structure can be expanded, by adding or substituting elements; more complex structures can be rearranged or simplified by removing elements. If essential elements are removed, the structure collapses.

In the simplest English structure, a single noun precedes a verb:

Teenagers upset me.

But other elements can take the place of a noun. In the examples above, the basic structure remains intact in all the changes.

The noun can be replaced by a pronoun:

They upset me.

Or by a noun phrase:

Their refusal to move upset me.

Or by a noun clause:

Leaving lights on upsets me.

The technical terms for these other elements all share the word 'noun', precisely because they have the same function in the structure. (See Chapters 7, 8 and 9 on phrase and clause structure). Thus the basic structure of noun + verb remains constant. This analogy with construction games forms the basis for the teaching approach to grammar, used in Section 1.

Approach to teaching grammar

Perhaps the most important aspect of the teaching approach is that it is based on language users' intuitive awareness of what is – or is not – grammatical. The activities in the book provide examples that can be used in the classroom. These activities invite the reader to use their implicit understanding of structure to develop confidence in the use of explicit terminology.

In conjunction with this is the use of authentic examples of language use, wherever possible. These are taken from a variety of sources, including literary and non-literary genres, contemporary and older texts. This provides breadth of study, encouraging pupils' exploration of a diversity of styles and showing the flexibility of language use in a variety of contexts.

Another important aspect of the approach used is that it is based on interaction with texts, in the belief that people learn best when they are actively engaged. Many activities are 'playful', for the reasons, and in the ways, described by Crystal in his book *Language Play* (1998: 187):

1   Children are used to playing with language, and encounter language play all around them.

2   Language play chiefly involves manipulating language structures.

3   A major aim is to improve children's ability with language structures. Therefore:

4   We should make use of their abilities in language play.

The type of 'play' used in the activities can be compared to construction games such as Jenga, mentioned above. This active manipulation of structures is also based on the fundamental principles of grammar analysis. The academic terms used are: 'substitution', 'deletion', 'insertion' and 'transposition'. These are 'basic' in the sense that they are fundamental to the system of grammatical classification. Luckily, they are also basic in the sense of being simple to understand. The concepts can be explained in more concrete terms, and provide tools for pupils to use in direct, active exploration of grammatical concepts.

TABLE 1.2 The four tests

Substitution	See if you can take out one part of the structure and replace it with another. If so, the substituted part must have a similar function.
Deletion	See if you can remove some parts of the structure. This will show whether these are optional, or essential, elements.
Insertion	See if you can add extra parts to the structure. This will also show that these are optional elements.
Transposition	See whether you can move some parts to other positions in the structure. This will show which are the movable elements.

The use of these four principles leads to the final important aspect of the approach.

Form vs function

This approach to grammar emphasises the **function** of words, phrases and clauses, as pupils develop understanding of the ways that parts of the structure operate in relation to each other. At Key Stages 3 and 4, the Framework emphasises the importance of consolidating their understanding of the roles of words.

As each term is introduced in Section 1, confidence is developed by exploration of its function. This focus on role – or function – is a more reliable way of understanding concepts such as noun, verb, adverb and subordinate clause, which may have been introduced earlier, using definitions based on their meaning or form.

> **Year 7:** understand and have the terminology to describe the role of word classes

Grammatical explanations based on **meaning** are a familiar memory for most people:

- A noun is a naming word.
- A verb is a doing/action word.
- An adjective is a describing word.

Sadly, these quick definitions only help with the most obvious examples; authentic language use rarely provides clear-cut, textbook examples. For example, which are the 'doing words' in this sentence?

There was a deafening scream as the twister began its plunging descent.

It would be reasonable to say that the words 'deafening', 'scream', 'twister', 'plunging', 'descent' are 'doing' words, as they suggest actions. However, the verbs are 'was' and began', neither of which convey much action.

Which are the 'describing words' in this sentence?

The drunk tottered into the alley, clutching a bottle of vodka under his raincoat.

There are no adjectives in this sentence, yet description is conveyed by nouns – 'drunk', 'alley', 'vodka', 'raincoat' – or the verbs – 'tottered', 'clutching'.

Another approach is to define word classes by the **form** of words. For example, an adverb is a word that ends in '–ly'. This also works only for classic, textbook examples. This is because of the changing nature of the English language. (See Chapters 4–6).

Unlike languages such as Latin, French and Spanish, modern English language no longer uses many inflections, i.e. changing the form of words by adding suffixes. Pupils should be aware that the same 'letter string' may function in different ways. For example, the form of the word 'light' remains identical in the following sentences, but its role changes.

What word class is 'light'?

This is a <u>light</u> suitcase.
I always travel <u>light</u>.
Have you got a <u>light</u>?
<u>Light</u> my fire.

The approach in Section 1 explores the function of grammatical concepts, by using the four tests outlined above. Their use is demonstrated briefly as a way of clarifying the role of word classes and consolidating the terminology.

Substitution can be used to make the function of a particular word clear, by replacing it by more familiar examples of the word class in question. For example,

This is a <u>lovely/nice</u> suitcase.	*(functions as)*	*adjective*
I always travel <u>carefully/wisely/cheaply</u>.	*(functions as)*	*adverb*
Have you got <u>any money/my book/a car</u>?	*(functions as)*	*noun*
<u>Extinguish/enjoy/report</u> the fire.	*(functions as)*	*verb*

Deletion can be used to show if a word functions as an adjective or adverb, as these are usually optional extras. Nouns, verbs, prepositions, etc. cannot be deleted. The following example shows which words can, and cannot, be deleted.

This is a (<u>light</u>) suitcase.	*adjective deleted*
I always travel (<u>light</u>).	*adverb deleted*
Have you got a <u>light</u>?	*noun cannot be deleted*
<u>Light</u> my fire.	*verb cannot be deleted*

NB The word 'always' can also be deleted and therefore functions as an adjective or adverb. Substitution tests – 'usually / rarely / often / never' – suggest it is an adverb, because of the '–ly' forms.

The other tests can be demonstrated in a further example:

My neighbours play music.

Insertion can be used as a test for adjectives and adverbs (see Chapter 6). One or more adjectives can be inserted before nouns.

(<u>annoying young</u>)		(<u>vile modern</u>)	
My	*neighbours play*		*music.*

Adverbs can be inserted in a variety of positions: before or after verbs, at the beginning or end of sentences.

	(<u>often</u>)	(<u>loudly</u>)
The neighbours	*play music.*	

Adverbs can also be inserted before adjectives, or other adverbs:

This is an <u>extremely</u> light suitcase.
The neighbours <u>very often</u> play music loudly.

Transposition is a useful test for adverbs, or adverbial phrases or clauses.

Adverbs can often be moved to other positions in the structure.

> *I travel <u>light always</u>.*
> *I travel light <u>when I go on holiday</u>.*
>
> <u>*Often*</u> *the neighbours <u>loudly</u> play music.*
> <u>*At weekends*</u> *the neighbours play music <u>loudly</u>.*

Summary

The approach to grammar teaching and learning in this book can be summarised:

- It is descriptive, rather than prescriptive.
- It explores a variety of authentic language use.
- It is based on intuitive understanding.
- Language structure is seen as three-dimensional.
- It emphasises the role (or function) of elements of structure with meaning and form as subsidiary.
- It uses 'playful' activities based on four tests.

A final word on the debate about English education – whether knowing about structure or using language is more effective. A recent study at the University of York (2005) suggests that grammar teaching has little impact on pupils' ability to use the language. The writer Phillip Pullman tends to support their conclusions, in 2005 characterising the essential activity for children as being 'playful' with language:

> Fooling about, playing with it, pushing it this way and that, turning it sideways, painting it different colours, looking at it from the back, putting one thing on top of another, asking silly questions, mixing things up, making absurd comparisons, discovering unexpected similarities, making pretty patterns, and all the time saying 'Supposing...I wonder... What if...'
>
> (www.guardian.co.uk)

Yet the activities he describes are surely explorations into the structure of language. I believe that there is no need to choose either structure or use. Playing with – or using language – is not distinct from learning about language, but a means of doing so.

The layout of the book

- A list of key terms is provided at the beginning of each section. These are highlighted in bold when they first occur in the following text.
- References to the Framework for Teaching English at Key Stages 3 and 4 are provided in marginal boxes, as well as cross-references to other chapters and pages in the book.

- Boxes highlighting intriguing examples appear throughout the book.
- Activities are numbered and the accompanying CD provides commentaries on these. Please note that some activities require no commentary.
- References to published works provide the author's surname and date, with full details in the bibliography at the end of the book.

2

The building blocks of language

The book begins with the smallest unit of grammar – the structure of words.

TABLE 2.1 Levels of structure

One or more **morphemes**	combine to form	words.
One or more **words**	combine to form	phrases.
One or more **phrases**	combine to form	clauses.
One or more **clauses**	combine to form	sentences.
One or more **sentences**	combine to form	paragraphs and whole texts.

Although it might seem that a word is the basic unit of language, many can be broken down into smaller elements. For example, the words 'smaller' and 'elements' both have a familiar word at the core, plus an ending that adds to the meaning:

small + –er
element + –s

The technical term for the smallest meaningful unit of language is a morpheme.

Everyone understands this at an intuitive level. Even infants show their understanding of morphology, when they create forms like 'goed' or 'foots'. We are able to use words without wondering where they came from, or how they were formed. As the National Literacy Strategy (2004) comments, 'The uncertainty for teachers is how far to make this knowledge explicit.' So what are the benefits of providing pupils with terminology?

The study of morphology encourages pupils to notice words. Their knowledge of the structure and origins of English words can be applied to skills required in the National Curriculum programme of study.

Language variation

Pupils should be taught about how language varies, including:

- the importance of standard English as the language of public communication nationally and often internationally
- attitudes to language use
- the development of English, including changes over time, borrowings from other languages, origins of words, and the impact of electronic communication on written language.

> **Year 7:** draw on analogies to known words, roots, derivations, word families, morphology and familiar spelling patterns
>
> **Year 7:** work out the meaning of unknown words using context, etymology, morphology, compound patterns
>
> **Year 7:** investigate and apply lexical patterns, e.g. adding '–ify' to an adjective to create a verb

In the Framework for Key Stages 3 and 4, the most obvious applications are listed at Word level for spelling and vocabulary.

Section 1 of this book began with the wider issues: attitudes to standard and non-standard English; varying degrees of formality in different situations. It then explored the principles of word formation and the origins of English words. This chapter shows applications of this knowledge to reading skills and spelling.

Language variation

This section explores attitudes to words in the language, introducing the concepts of a standard language and language variation. The notion of standard English is often seen as a straightforward issue for teaching: some forms of language are 'proper' and 'correct', and others are not. However, the Key Stage Strategy consistently links the terms 'standard English' and 'language variation', acknowledging more complexity in language use. The choice of lower case – rather than a capital letter – in their use of the term 'standard English' is significant, as it suggests a more tentative attitude, rather than the notion of a fixed, absolute standard.

Non-standard forms, such as dialect and slang, are no longer regarded as 'incorrect' or 'ungrammatical'. However, this does not mean – as some debates in the media suggest – that 'anything' goes! Pupils must be able to use standard English in formal situations.

Key words

slang   colloquial   standard English   non-standard   language variation/variety
language change   formality   formal   informal   situation/context/circumstances
genre   purpose   audience   topic   writer

Language in use

Why are you dissing me?
Eminem complained that Nicole Kidman dissed him, but he disses his mother in songs.

What is slang?

How do you respond to the use of 'diss' in these quotations? Is this type of language **slang**? Not a proper word? Another sign of the sloppy way teenagers use language? Or of the dreadful influence of Americanisms?

In any language, the standard variety is regarded as having a special social status. **Standard English**, therefore, is the model for educated written usage. But language is not static. The linguist and writer Stephen Pinker commented in an online chat:

> As far as I know, all languages have slang. Indeed lots of standard words started out life as slang, such as 'mob,' 'fun,' and 'bully.' Even today, slang words such as 'to flame' and 'to diss' are coming into the mainstream. No doubt that happens in all languages, because words are not designed by committees, but have to be with a creative speaker who first coins the word.
>
> (www. wordsmith.org)

As Pinker points out, much language that is considered standard English now began as slang usage. Dictionaries record words that have come into the 'mainstream' of language use, and indicate whether a word is considered slang or **colloquial** (abbreviated to 'colloq.') rather than standard. Pupils should be aware of the date of the dictionary used, as language changes each year.

Activity 2.1

- Look up these words in a concise dictionary:
    bully
    mob
    fun
    diss
- Where do they come from?
- Are they considered slang or colloquial?

Attitudes to language variation

The previous activity showed how attitudes to words change over time. When the abbreviation 'mob' was first used for a disorderly crowd, it would have been considered **non-standard**, but it is now a standard English word. It is frequently the younger generation that introduce new words – with the unfavourable reactions noted by the American linguist John McWhorter (1998):

> We cannot stop language from changing, and so there will always be things that 'people are saying lately.' The people reinterpreting the language will naturally tend to be young, and thus high-spirited and flippant, but we must not let this mislead us into thinking of

the innovations as rambunctious 'breaking of rules,' because this is the sole way language has been changing since time immemorial.

It is important – especially for teachers working with pupils in a diverse and changing world – not to take a purist stance on **language variety** and **change**. As the philologist Weekley (1929) states, 'Stability in language is synonymous with *rigor mortis.'*

However, it is equally important to point out to pupils the effects of non-standard forms. Walter Raleigh (1926) makes this pertinent point:

> The strong vivid slang word cannot be counted on to do its work. It sets the hearer thinking, not on the subject of my speech, but on such irrelevant questions as the nature of my past education and the company I keep.

Activity 2.2

- Note the choice of vocabulary in this extract from a literature essay.
- Does it distract the reader from the ideas expressed?

> *Lady Macbeth is such a high-maintenance wife, it's no wonder Macbeth was driven to murder Donald, but should he have taken the rap for it? We can see in the play how she is constantly egging her husband on for her own ends. She calls him out for a coward and even makes jibes about his sexuality. This probably damages his ego so much that he can't stand up to her. He starts to believe that if he shows any fear, she'll take it as a sign that he's not really a man. She's the sort of female who will use unfair means to get what she wants. He is the sort of insecure man who falls for her tactics.*

Varying degrees of formality

The concept of **formality** is essential for the understanding of **language variation**, but needs some clarification. In everyday language, the word 'formality' means roughly the same as 'formal', indicating the type of behaviour, clothes or language suitable for public, ceremonial occasions. In language study, the term has a precise definition: 'the ways language use varies according to the situation'.

Thus it refers to a range of language use, including **informal** styles, as well as **formal**.

Pupils should be aware of different **situations** for language use, and the way that language varies according to these factors:

- **genre** – the text type, including forms of spoken, as well as written language
- **purpose** – what is the writer/speaker trying to achieve?
- **audience** – who is the intended reader/listener?

NB The Framework uses the terms '**context**' or '**circumstances**', as well as 'situation.'

Pupils are influenced by the language they encounter: predominantly spoken language and informal writing. Their use of such non-standard forms in other situations is often accidental and inappropriate. An activity, such as Activity 2.3 asks pupils to notice how 'youth-speak' is deliberately used for a particular situation. The paradox is that the text is written by a highly educated professional, whereas young pupils are usually required to adopt educated, professional styles of writing.

Activity 2.3

- Identify the non-standard word forms in the following text:
  - slang and colloquialisms
  - neologisms (new/invented words)
  - abbreviations
  - phonetic spellings (words spelled as pronounced).
- Describe the situation: genre, audience, purpose.
- What degree of formality is appropriate for this situation?

> *Welcome to the latest, brightest, most brilliant edition of* Bliss. *And have we got a top issue for you! Firstly, have you checked out our hair book? It's designed to make sure that even though you're probably back in daggy college gear, your hair will still be on top form. And just to make sure your life is a back-to-school depression-free zone,* Bliss' *Jo and Jenny have been scouring the world for seven of the most babelicious new boys we could find.*
>
> *On a sadder note, our Art Ed, Bill, has left to become a currazy freelance designer – so good luck Bill! But it's hallo to Phil Chill, our cool, new office DJ (and sub) who's been playing loads of ace toons to keep the office rockin'.*
>
> *Enjoy the issue.*
> *Dawn*
>
> *Editorial from* Bliss *magazine (1999)*

Genre, purpose and audience

The use of non-standard forms can be effective, if pupils are aware of the conventions associated with various situations. For example, the use of slang and colloquial forms is effective in **genres**, where a lively, personal voice is needed: talk with friends, dialogue in stories and drama, a first-person narrative.

The **purpose** of a piece of writing affects the degree of formality. Writing to inform usually requires a more formal tone, using standard English to ensure clarity of content. Writing to advise or persuade may benefit from a colloquial voice, but the tone needs to retain some authority, which might be lessened by the use of slang.

Consideration of the **audience** also influences formality. The use of slang can identify an in-group with shared interests. Although the use of standard English is the established convention for public communication, we can note some changes in attitudes. There is a trend towards increasing informality in some forms of public speaking and writing. The *Guardian* newspaper, for example, used the headline:

> *The boy done good!*

But the novice writer should be cautious about such innovation. Informality is restricted to certain **topics** – leisure pursuits, rather than serious news. The status of the **writer** is also a factor; where the credentials of the writer are well established, the use of slang is accepted as a deliberate, rather than lack of skill. However, pupils are encouraged to 'use imaginative vocabulary', 'exploit choice of language to achieve particular effects and appeal to the reader' and 'use language to gain attention'. The next section looks at the structure of words in more detail.

Word formation

This section introduces key terms that pupils need for the study of word formation. In order to understand the units that make up words, pupils need to distinguish between letters, phonemes and morphemes.

NB A box □ indicates an element of word structure. An asterisk (*) denotes structures that are not acceptable in English. A question mark (?) indicates some doubt over whether it is an acceptable word.

Key words
morphology   morpheme   letter   phoneme   syllable   word   root
stem   suffix   prefix

What is a morpheme?

The Greek root of the word 'morphology' sounds daunting, but some people may remember the cartoon character Morph – a plasticine figure that could change its form. A similar idea is conveyed by words like 'metamorphosis', from the Greek word *morphe*, meaning 'form', and *meta*, meaning 'after' or 'beyond'. The new words 'morph' and 'morphing' are now in contemporary language to suggest changing one thing smoothly into another. (**NB** The similar word 'morphine', however, comes from Latin *Morpheus*, the god of sleep.)

So, a **morpheme** is a form, unit or shape, and **morphology** is the study of the ways these units can be grouped together into a larger form. The idea of change is also relevant, as morphemes can be moved around (inserted, deleted and transposed) to change the structure and meanings of words. To clarify the precise definition of 'morpheme' as both the smallest and a meaningful unit, we can relate it to more familiar terms and concepts: letters, sounds, syllables, words.

Letters, or **phonemes**, are contenders for the smallest unit of language, but they are not meaningful. The letters 'p' 'i' and 'n' mean nothing in isolation. Nor do the individual sounds – phonemes: /p/ /i/ /n/.

Words may seem like the basic meaningful units: many words like 'pin' cannot be divided further. But if you take a more complex word like 'replaceable', it is clear that it can be broken down into smaller parts.

Syllables are the familiar way of dividing a word into smaller parts – the beats that make up the rhythm of a word, often exploited in poetry. The word 'replaceable' has four syllables, for example:

> *re-place-a-ble*

But not all syllables convey meaning, such as 'a' and 'ble'.

Deletion test

The grammatical test of deletion can be used to show which units of structure are meaningful, i.e. morphemes. If we apply the test of deletion to the structure of the word 'replaceable', we see that some parts of the word can be removed, leaving a meaningful form:

> *replace* able

> re *placeable*

> re *place* able

This shows that the word is formed from three morphemes:

re	place	able
(meaning 'again')	(the core meaning)	(meaning 'ability')

We cannot delete any letter, or even syllable:

> * *replaceabl* e

> * *replacea* ble

Thus a morpheme is *not* the same as a syllable. This distinction is tricky, as many morphemes are also single syllables. Activity 2.4 provides examples to explore the difference.

Types of morpheme

The Framework uses the terms **root** or **stem** for the part of the word that conveys the core meaning and can stand alone. The term **suffix** is used for morphemes that cannot stand alone, but are added to the end of words; whereas a **prefix** is a morpheme added to the beginning of a word.

Thus the structure of the word 'replaceable' can be analysed like this:

place	*stem/root*
re–	*prefix*
–able	*suffix*

NB Some textbooks use the terms 'free' and 'bound' morpheme for this distinction. The general term 'affix' refers to any bound morphemes. Apart from prefixes and suffixes, there are two other types of affix possible in word formation. As they are not commonly used in the formation of words in English, the terms are mentioned briefly:

circumfix	*an element added around the word structure*
infix	*an element added inside the word structure*

There are a few examples of infixes in non-standard contemporary English. These insert taboo words, e.g. 'abso-bloody-lutely'.

The following activity provides practice in identifying the structure of words. The pairs of words have similar syllables at the beginning or end. The deletion test shows whether these are morphemes – meaningful units.

Activity 2.4

■ Which words are formed from more than one morpheme?

■ Which morpheme is the root, or stem?

■ Which morpheme cannot stand alone – prefix or suffix?

TABLE 2.2

teacher	tiger	under	undo	rely	really
ceiling	painting	prise	itemise	prism	communism
terrible	dribble	defy	magnify	elephant	eject

Application to language variation

Year 8: collect and comment on examples of language change

The concept of bound morphemes – prefixes and suffixes – can be used when exploring language change and variation.

For example, the use of 'diss' (as in 'Don't diss me') shows a creative use of language, forming a free-standing new word from the prefix used in words such as:

dis–respect
dis–like
dis–agree

This may seem like flagrant breaking of the rules of English grammar, but is based on the principles of word formation. The same process has created these words:

hyper	*as in*	*hyperventilation*
mega	*as in*	*megawatt*
retro	*as in*	*retrograde*
pseud(o)	*as in*	*pseudopod*

Once only occurring as prefixes in scientific words, these are now used as free-standing words in colloquial usage. Attitudes to new word forms tend to change, as their use spreads into more 'respected' forms of language. The concepts of root, prefix and suffix will be used in the next section to explore the various patterns of words in English.

Identify lexical patterns

All words were 'new' at one time. This section emphasises the creative aspect of language use, and pupils' intuitive grasp of the principles by which meanings are conveyed. The key terms for types of word structure are introduced.

Key words

neologism   word family   inflection   derivation   compound
blending   abbreviation   acronym   onomatopoeia   clipping   back-formation

---

Language in use

I've got a feeling of fullupness.
Is a serious illness a killness?
My beamish boy... He chortled in his joy.
Roadrage and bluejacking on the increase.

Creating words

Young children are excellent sources of **neologisms** (newly created words), as are poets and journalists. The new words are rarely created 'out of the blue', but formed from existing morphemes. In the first example above, a child joins three morphemes to create a new noun, 'fullupness'. The second blends the two words 'kill' and 'illness' to convey the idea of a fatal illness. In his poem 'The Jabberwocky', Lewis Carroll created many 'nonsense' words that are strangely meaningful: 'beamish' seems like an adjective formed from the stem 'beam'. One blend of the words 'chuckle' and 'snort' – 'chortle' – has passed into standard

English. The new word 'roadrage' is now accepted, but many created words, such as 'bluejacking' (for the sending of offensive text messages) do not pass into standard usage. David Crystal (1995), explains the term for this:

> A nonce word (from the 16th-century phrase *for the nonce*, meaning 'for the once') is a lexeme created for temporary use, to solve an immediate problem of communications. Someone attempting to describe the excess water on a road after a storm was heard to call it a *fluddle* – she meant something bigger than a puddle but smaller than a flood. The newborn lexeme was forgotten (except by a passing linguist) almost as soon as it was spoken. It was obvious from the jocularly apologetic way in which the person spoke that she did not consider *fluddle* to be a 'proper' word at all. There was no intention to propose it for inclusion in a dictionary. As far as she was concerned, it was simply that there seemed to be no word in the language for what she wanted to say, so she made one up, for the nonce. In everyday conversation, people create nonce-words like this all the time.

NB Some linguists prefer to use the term 'lexeme' instead of word, to cover the range of forms that a single word may have: 'walk', 'walks', 'walking', 'walked'. In this book, I will use the term 'word' for clarity and simplicity.

Word families

Language users can both create new words and understand unfamiliar words, by making connections with other related words. A group of words that share the same root, or stem, is called a **word family**. For example, the words 'magnificent', 'magnitude', 'magnate', 'magnum opus' are all formed from the Latin root *magnus*. Even without a knowledge of Latin, it is possible to work out that all share the meaning of 'large'. Other families of words share the same prefix ('repeat', 'return', 'redo') or suffix ('readable', 'passable', 'doable').

Pupils' intuitive understanding of morphology can be demonstrated in creative activities of word formation, such as the following:

Activity 2.5

- List existing words with 'chew' as the root, e.g. 'chews', 'chewing'.
- How do you interpret the meaning of words, e.g. 'prechew', 'rechewable'?
- Invent some other words with 'chew' as the root.
- Supply your own definition. Check to see how others interpret the meaning.

Processes of word formation

Not only do users instinctively choose prefixes for the beginnings of words and suffixes for the endings; they order more than one affix according to the rules of English morphology. They understand implicitly that there is no scope for *transposition* – morphemes cannot be moved from one place to another in the structure of English words. For example, a complex word like 'un-re-chew-abil-ity' is felt to be 'grammatical', whereas the following are not:

* abil-chew-ity
* re-un-chew-able

Pupils should know the terms for different processes of word formation in the English language. This knowledge can be applied to grammar, as well as to reading and spelling. The addition of prefixes and suffixes to roots is the most common lexical pattern. Most words in English are formed by the process of inflection and derivation.

Inflection

Inflection refers to suffixes marking grammatical forms such as plurals and verb tenses.

–s marks the plural form of most nouns ('tables')
–s also marks the third person of verbs ('jumps')
–ing marks the progressive form of verbs ('jumping')
–ed marks the past tense of verbs ('jumped')

Modern English language has relatively few inflections in comparison with other languages. There is little scope for creativity in grammatical inflections, but some changes have occurred over time. In earlier periods, English used more inflections for verbs, e.g. 'goeth' and 'goest', which have been lost in a process of simplification.

Year 8: draw on their knowledge of other languages to identify some of the similarities and differences between those languages and English

This has not happened in Romance languages that are derived almost exclusively from Latin. For example, the Italian verb meaning 'speak' has dozens of endings for person and tense:

Year 9: investigate ways English has changed over time

parlo, parli, parle, parliamo, parlisti, parlaron, parlavo, parlando, etc.

These languages have inflections for the gender of nouns. German also has inflections for the case (whether subject, object, etc.) of nouns.

In contrast, inflections that indicate case only occur in pronouns in English:

I, me, my, mine

English uses few inflections for nouns, apart from pluralisation. This is normally '–s' suffix, but the older form: '–en' remains in a few exceptions:

children, oxen

The suffix '–ess' is used on some nouns to indicate gender:

actress, waitress, manageress

The suffix '–ette' indicates diminutive size:

cigarette, laundrette, usherette

NB Gender suffixes tend to be avoided in contemporary language use, because they mark the masculine form as the norm, implying that the female version is subsidiary and – in the example of 'usherette' – actually smaller.

Suffixes '–er' and '–est' are added to adjectives, to indicate comparative and superlative:

> *big, bigger, biggest*

Derivation

The process of **derivation** also uses the addition of prefixes and suffixes. Many existing affixes are used to form words with new meanings:

> *pre-shrunk*
> *clean-able*
> *anti-static*

Some suffixes indicate a change in word class:

> *beam (verb)*   *beamish (adjective)*
> *happy (adjective)*   *happiness (noun)*
> *create (verb)*   *creation (noun)*

Proper nouns can also be used more widely, by the process of inflection and derivation:

> *hoovering*   *from the brand name Hoover*
> *sellotatape*   *from Sellotape*
> *thatcherite*   *from the person's name (Mrs Thatcher)*
> *macjob*   *from the company name (McDonald's)*

Pupils' knowledge of inflection and derivation can be used in the study of syntax. (See Chapter 4 on word classes and Chapter 8 on verb phrases)

Compounding

This process is also very common, accounting for a high percentage of new words, formed by joining two words:

> *roadrage*   *road + rage*
> *airport*   *air + port*
> *coursework*   *course + work*

(See Chapter 3 on spelling for further discussion of language change with regard to the use of hyphens).

Both **compounding** and inflection or derivation can be used to form words:

> *fullupness*   *full + up + ness*
> *bluejacking*   *blue + jack + ing*
> *signposting*   *sign + post + ing*

In some cases, usually colloquial, three words are joined:

bad-for-you
in-your-face

Blending

Blending is a type of compounding – both shortening and combining two words. It tends to occur in playful uses of language, with a few examples passing into mainstream usage.

chortle	*chuckle + snort*
killness	*kill + illness*
motel	*motor + hotel*
chunnel	*channel + tunnel*
slackademic	*slacker + academic*
rockabilly	*rock and roll + hillbilly*

Abbreviation

This process is common, with the simpler **abbreviation** often passing into standard usage and the original form being lost.

fridge	*from refrigerator*
bus	*from omnibus*
pram	*from perambulator*

Some words are formed by a combination of abbreviation plus derivation or compounding:

high-tech, celeb-wise, sitcom

NB The term **clipping** is used in some books for this type of shortening of words. The term **back-formation** refers to a few words whose original form has been abbreviated, as if it contained a suffix. This process would not be noticed without knowledge of the history of the English language.

burgle	*a burglar (from Old French* burgier *– to pillage)*
letch/lech	*a letcher (from Old French* lechier *– to live in debauchery)*

Acronym

The use of initial letters of a phrase to form a word is very common in organisations. Only those **acroynms** of use to a wider group pass into the standard language:

GCSE	*General Certificate of Secondary Education*
LASER	*Light Amplification by the Stimulated Emission of Radiation*
BANANA	*Build Absolutely Nothing Anywhere Near Anything*

Onomatopoeia

Some words are simply invented, the sound of the word resembling its meaning (**onomatopoeia**). In dictionaries, their origin is noted as 'imitative':

> *clatter*
> *bling-bling*

These terms for the processes of word formation can be practised in activities such as the following:

Activity 2.6

- What processes were used in the formation of these words?

> **Language in use**
>
> babelicious   fanzine   telethon   chocaholic   mike   blog   lad mag   Cheriegate
> fitnesswise   malformed   homesick   AIDS   bloodthirsty   demigod   rustle

Application to language change

Year 8: collect and comment on examples of language change, e.g. new words associated with electronic communication and ICT

This knowledge of processes of word formation can also be applied to language change.

The language of new technologies is a source of creative word formation. The language of the media also uses innovative word choice, as the next activity shows:

Activity 2.7

The following compounds all occurred in an edition of the magazine *Just 17*.

- Even if you have never seen the compound used before, is the meaning understood?
- Which ones are listed in a contemporary dictionary?

	seen before	understand	in dictionary
well-busy			
matchmaker			
tiptop			
chat-up			
close-knit			

bad-for-you
catwalk
half-decent
work experience
knock-out
giveaway
closed-circuit
sell-out
factfile
streetwise
wise-up

The next section looks at the origins of English, and shows how many words have come into the language by a process of borrowing from other languages.

The origins of English

In the words of the film *Life of Brian*,

> Apart from the sanitation, medicine, education, wine, public order, irrigation, roads, the fresh water system and public health, what have the Romans ever done for us?!

The Roman invasion of Britain introduced, not only the advantages mentioned above, but a large store of vocabulary. Many more Latin words came into the English language, via French, in the 300 years of Norman rule after the Battle of Hastings in 1066. This period of language is termed Middle English. Around this time, many words were also adopted from Greek, via Latin. Pupils should: have some understanding of the origins of words in English; recognise links between words related by word families and roots; and work out the meanings of unknown words or use dictionaries.

Key words
etymology   Latin (L)   Greek (Gr)   French (Fr)   Old Norse (ON)
Old English (OE)   borrowing

> **Language in use**
>
> *The would-be ingangers from France were smitten hip and thigh and our tongue remained selfthrough and strong, unbecluttered and unbedizened with outlandish Latin-born words of French outshoot... The craft and insight of our Anglish tongue for the more cunning switchmeangroups, for unthingsome and overthingsome withtakings, gives a matchless tool to bards, deep thinkers and trypiecemen.*

Old English

In 1966, the comic writer Paul Jennings wrote how English might have been if William the Conqueror had been defeated at the Clash of Hastings (the word 'battle' has its origins in the Latin verb meaning 'to beat'). A text avoiding any words of Latin, French or Greek origin sounds strange. Going back to the earliest roots of the English language, we find terms for basic concepts, but this does not make the text simple to understand.

Many of the basic words in English are of Anglo-Saxon/Germanic (termed **Old English**) origin. These words are often monosyllables:

> *meat, wife, sun*

But more complex concepts could be conveyed by combining words, as in the invented terms in Jennings' article:

overthingsome	*metaphysical*	*unbecluttered*
selfthrough	*uncontaminated*	*unbedizened*
switchmeangroup	*metaphor*	*inganger*
trypieceman	*essayist*	*unthingsome*
withtaking	*concept*	

The history of the English language can be traced further back to Celtic origins. However, very few Celtic words remain, mostly in place names or for geographical features.

> *pen*   *meaning 'hill' (as in Penrith)*

The Viking invasion introduced words from **Old Norse**. These are often also monosyllables:

> *get, give, hit, kick, law, take, they, want, window*

Interestingly, many words of Norse origin can be recognised, as they begin with a 'sk' sound:

> *scatter, score, scowl, scrape, scrub, sister, skill, skin, skirt, sky*

In the early history of English, the language was affected by invasions from other cultures. In more recent centuries, the reverse has been more influential: travel, trade and colonisation all introduced new words into English. The increasing power of the English-speaking nations (including their media and technology) has affected other languages. As the Canadian journalist Mark Abley (2003) suggests:

> Modern English is the Wal-Mart of languages: convenient, huge, hard to avoid, superficially friendly, and devouring all rivals in its eagerness to expand.

The **etymology**, or origin, of words is given – even in concise dictionaries – in square brackets at the end of the definition. If abbreviations are used, these are listed at the beginning of the dictionary: **L – Latin**; **Gr – Greek**; OE – Old English; ON – Old Norse; **Fr – French**; etc.

Year 9: make use of different kinds of dictionary

The next activity shows the process of **borrowing** from many other languages.

Activity 2.8

Use a dictionary to check the sources of the words underlined in this text.

She chucked a banana, chocolate and a cardigan into her duffel bag, suspecting that leotards would alarm the guy she'd agreed to meet in the spa. His blurb didn't augur well, she had to admit. 'Gothic gentleman seeks bewitching redhead into bourbon.' He sounded too highbrow for her, probably the sort who stunk of cologne and wore a cravat. Frankly she was more likely to go for a 'daredevil maverick who craves hooch'.

The next chapter shows how pupils' understanding of morphology can be applied to the skills of reading and spelling.

3

Applications of morphology

This chapter shows how pupils' knowledge of morphology can be applied to Word-level skills. The first section uses awareness of roots, prefixes and suffixes to develop understanding of unfamiliar vocabulary. The second section suggests some applications to spelling.

Applications to reading

Key words
generative words   key words

Language in use
Paediatrician's house stoned by angry mob.   *Anti-natal classes?*

Prefixes and suffixes

Year 7: work out the meaning of unknown words using context, etymology, morphology

Efficient readers do not need to turn to a dictionary every time an unfamiliar word occurs. Apart from using guesswork from the context of the word, the ability to break down the word into meaningful parts helps to work out the meaning. This skill can be developed by understanding the meaning of prefixes and suffixes. In addition, the meaning of common roots from Latin and Greek is an aid. Of course, nothing in language is ever completely straightforward. Partial (mis)understanding leads to the unfortunate confusions between 'paedophile' and 'paediatrician', and between 'ante–' (before) and 'anti–' (against).

There are tens of thousands of words in the English language. These are formed from a smaller number of prefixes, suffixes and roots, but a full list would overwhelm any student of English. Paolo Friere's work on literacy in Brazil has been influential in many ways. The first principle is to begin with the vocabulary of the group or community. Freire (1973) believed that **generative words** should have special affective importance to learners and should evoke the social, cultural and political contexts in which learners use them. Then generative words are chosen to show how elements can be separated and recombined to form other words. According to Freire (1970), in Portuguese only 15 words are needed to generate all the other words in the language.

In the English language, Brown (1971) suggests there are 14 words that contain the 20 most useful prefixes and the 14 most important roots, which are to be found in over 14,000 words in a concise dictionary or close to 100,000 words in an unabridged dictionary size. However, his **key words** (such as 'oversufficient') are unlikely to engage the interest of school students.

Roots

I list some of Brown's roots below, adding some others of potential usefulness:

tend	*to stretch*
spec	*to look at*
fac	*to make*
duct	*to lead*
scrib	*to write*
mit	*to send*
pos	*to place*
cap	*to hold*
capit	*head*
corp	*body*
carn	*meat*
vert	*to turn*
ject	*to throw*
fort	*strong*
tract	*to drag*
noct	*night*
somn	*sleep*
pac	*peace*
mal	*bad*
ben	*good*

It is important to find a meaningful context for the study of key roots and prefixes. If we aim to engage pupils in dialogue and base learning in their own experience, teachers need to choose words that stimulate interest. The following activity draws on pupils' familiarity with brand names. These are usually invented words, which use awareness of existing roots to suggest the desired set of meanings.

> **Year 7:** draw on analogies to known words, roots, derivations, word families

Activity 3.1

- ■ If you saw these words on an advertisement poster, what sort of product would you think of?
  - *Jectox*
  - *Uni-Ductor*
  - *The Fortiffs*
  - *Tendene*
  - *Scribeasy*
  - *Spectaxis*
- ■ Identify the root of each word.
- ■ Collect other words with the same root – a word family.
- ■ Can you work out the meaning of the root?
- ■ Use a dictionary to check the origin of the words.

Language in use

Jectox might suggest a powerful cleaning fluid.

The root is *ject*.

Word family: 'eject', 'inject', 'project', 'reject', 'deject'

Ject means 'to throw', from the Latin word *jacere*.

Prefixes

Activity 3.1 showed how pupils can work out the meaning of unfamiliar words by understanding the meaning of key Latin roots. These are usually combined with prefixes. For example, the root '–vert', meaning 'to turn', occurs in a word family:

divert	*turn aside*
revert	*turn back*
convert	*turn together*
invert	*turn inwards*
pervert	*turn strangely?*

Hodges (1982) claims that there are 14 key prefixes, which account for the majority (82 per cent) of the 20,000 most-used English words. Pupils can develop their understanding of these prefixes by forming word families.

- Supply three or more examples of words with these key prefixes.
- Suggest a definition for each prefix (use a dictionary if you like).

> *com–*
>
> *dis–*
>
> *ex–*
>
> *in–*
>
> *pre–*
>
> *sub–*

Application to language change

Although academics have listed the most commonly used prefixes, it is interesting to note how some rare, technical terms have been adopted into colloquial language, not only the examples mentioned before – 'mega', 'hyper', 'retro', 'hyper', 'pseudo' – but also:

anti–	
ante–	*('to up the ante')*
auto–	
contra–	
homo–	
micro–	
macro–	
mini–	
tele–	
trans–	*('tranny')*
ultra–	

It seems that more obscure words and morphemes are greeted with delight, rather than trepidation. In this spirit, teachers might extend the range further:

ambi–	*on both sides, as in*	*ambidextrous, ambiguous*
proto–	*first, as in*	*protocol, prototype*

Suffixes

Some suffixes are useful in working out the meaning of words. Many of these are intuitively understood:

–arium	*a place, as in*	*aquarium, solarium*
–ify	*to make, as in*	*liquify, codify*
–itis	*diseases, as in*	*bronchitis, colitis*
–ee	*person affected by the action, as in*	*employee, addressee*

The suffix -ism can indicate a state in a neutral sense – 'baptism', but new words tend to include a negative connotation: 'ageism'.

–ism	*action, state, now pejorative, as in*	*alcoholism, racism*

The suffix -wise is an interesting example of language change. Once only found in words of Old English origin:

–wise	*way or manner, as in*	*clockwise, lengthwise*

it is now used to form new words, usually with connotations of popular psychology or business jargon, such as 'relationship-wise', 'profit-wise', 'viability-wise'.

Other suffixes are not so useful for decoding meaning, but will be useful in the study of the next level of language – word classes. They will also be used in some applications to spelling later in the chapter. These suffixes change a word from one class (type) to another, for example:

to nouns	*–age (from French)*	*reportage, spoilage*
to verbs	*–ate (from Latin)*	*aggravate, liquidate*
to adjectives	*–en (from Old English)*	*leaden, wooden*

These are the only two suffixes that change words into adverbs:

–ly	*quickly, really*
–wise	*likewise, clockwise*

(See Chapter 4 for further exploration of grammatical suffixes.)

Two last suffixes of interest for issues of 'correctness' and language change are the endings -um and -us on some nouns of Latin derivation. These suffixes were originally the singular form, with an inflection change in the plural:

(auto)bus	*? autobi*	*now always*	*buses*
syllabus	*? syllabi*	*now commonly*	*syllabuses*
corpus	*corpora*		*corpuses*
referendum	*referenda*		*referendums*
curriculum	*curricula*		*? curriculums*

The plural forms of these nouns of Latin origin are now used for both singular and plural, with the original singular form dropping out of use:

medium	*the media is/are*
datum	*the data is/are*

Awareness of suffixes can also help with some common spelling problems, outlined in the next section.

Applications to spelling

Spelling is a source of pride to those who can, and a source of embarrassment to those who can't. This section suggests strategies for pupils to address spelling difficulties.

Year 9: apply knowledge of word origins, families and morphology

Key words
phonic vowel consonant assimilation phoneme homonym hyphen schwa homograph homophone elision

Why is English spelling a problem?

Language in use

I'm raelly worierd abuot the delcine in good sllepping, and I'm not sure I even agere with the Cambirdge resaerch. I'd like to know mroe about the methodlogoy, the contorl grupps, the size of the smaple. And who kowns, it may just be anrother innernet joke. I've been saerchnig evreywerhe for the oriignal resaerch but I cna't fnid it. I even tried Goggle. Maybe I'm spelling Cambirge wrong.

This is the final paragraph of an 800-word article by Michael Johnson, written in 2003. Although nearly half the words are misspelled, it can be read and understood with little problem. As Johnson says,

> Accroding to the exprets, the eye deosn't need or evn want the whoole wrord. It noets the frist and last lettres, and fills in the rest by inrefence. You can even add or dorp lettres. The jumumble in btweeen is irrveralent. Cogintion hapneps vrey fast and quite misteriollusly.
> (www.guardian.co.uk)

However, the fact remains that spelling is assessed. It is a slight comfort to know of many successful people who are, or were, dyslexic: W. B. Yeats, Albert Einstein, Leonardo da Vinci, Winston Churchill, Richard Branson, Whoopi Goldberg, Eddie Izzard.

There is much controversy about the best way of teaching spelling: by exposure to the appearance of words, or by learning the sounds of letters that form words.

Year 7: sound out words phonemically

The **phonic** approach provides pupils with a strategy, but it is often unreliable. This is partly because the English language does not have a straightforward relationship between sounds and letters, but also because English is derived from various language origins.

There are 26 letters in the alphabet to represent 44 **phonemes** – meaningful sounds.

The 44 distinct sounds must be represented by various combinations of letters, rather than a simple one-to-one correlation, as in Italian, for example. Whereas Italian – and many other languages – derive from a single source, English has a number of different origins. The ways the letters are combined depends more on the language of origin, than any systematic rules. For example, the 'f' sound is spelled in different ways:

flaccid	*f*	*Latin*
gruff	*ff*	*Dutch*
enough	*gh*	*Old English*
photography	*ph*	*Greek*

Homonyms

It is not always the long, complex words that prove the most difficult to spell. Many short, common words are a problem, because they are so similar. The three related terms – **homonym, homograph, homophone** – all begin with the prefix 'homo', meaning 'same'. The overall term is 'homonym', which can be distinguished into two types of similarity:

Homograph – words with the same spelling, but a different meaning:

furniture polish/Polish people
a lead pencil/the dog's lead

Homophone – words with the same sound, but a different spelling and meaning:

read/reed
pair/pear
write/right/rite/wright

Vowels

The discrepancy between sounds and letters is mainly in the **vowels**. There are 5 letters (plus 'y') for vowels, but English uses 20 different vowel sounds. (See Chapter 11 on phonology.)

The following rhyme is used to alert EAL learners (of English as an Alternative Language) to the scope of the problem. It may also reassure native speakers who despair of ever getting to grips with spelling. If you read it aloud, you can see how words spelled in a similar way are pronounced differently.

When the English tongue we speak
Why is <u>break</u> not rhymed with <u>weak</u>?
Won't you tell me why it's true
We say <u>sew</u>, but also <u>few</u>?
And the maker of a verse
Cannot rhyme his <u>horse</u> with <u>worse</u>?
<u>Beard</u> is not the same as <u>heard</u>,
<u>Cord</u> is different from <u>word</u>,
<u>Cow</u> is cow, but <u>low</u> is low,
<u>Shoe</u> is never rhymed with <u>foe</u>.
Think of <u>hose</u> and <u>dose</u> and <u>lose</u>,

And think of <u>goose</u> and yet of <u>choose</u>,
Think of <u>comb</u> and <u>tomb</u> and <u>bomb</u>,
<u>Doll</u> and <u>roll</u> and <u>home</u> and <u>some</u>.
And since <u>pay</u> is rhymed with <u>say</u>,
Why not <u>paid</u> with <u>said</u> I pray?
Think of <u>blood</u> and <u>food</u> and <u>good</u>;
<u>Mould</u> is not pronounced like <u>could</u>.
Why is it <u>done</u>, but <u>gone</u> and <u>lone</u>-
Is there any reason known?
To sum it up, it seems to me
That sounds and letters don't agree.

The most common phoneme (or sound) in English has its own name – **schwa** – as well as a symbol- /ə/. This sound is made in the middle of the mouth and occurs in most unstressed syllables:

<u>a</u>part (schwa sound for the initial syllable)

This causes a problem for phonic approaches to spelling, as the schwa sound in unstressed syllables can be represented by various combinations of letters. For example:

a	comfort<u>a</u>ble
e	cin<u>e</u>ma
i	infin<u>i</u>te
io	capt<u>io</u>n

This aspect of English phonology causes some common misspellings, by using the letter 'e' as the closest representation of the schwa sound in the unstressed syllable:

* seperate	not pronounced	sep / ar / ate
* grammer	not pronounced	gramm / ar
* definate	not pronounced	de / fi / nite

Spelling strategies

Because of these irregularities, a phonic approach to spelling can only deal with words spelled as they are pronounced. There have been moves in the past to introduce a phonetic system of spelling: ITA – Initial Teaching Alphabet.

George Bernard Shaw left money in his will to promote a regular system of English spelling. His famous example to show the illogicality of English spelling was:

Question: What does 'G-H-O-T-I' spell?
Answer: Fish!

The sound	/f/	spelled	'gh' as in	enough
The sound	/i/	spelled	'o' as in	women
The sound	/sh/	spelled	'ti' as in	station

But this attempt to simplify spelling went out of favour.

Many people find that they have a photographic sense of the appearance of the whole word and, while they cannot spell a word out letter by letter, they can tell whether it looks right. This leads to a word recognition approach, sometimes based on flash cards, but more often on providing as much exposure as possible to the written word in context.

Year 7: make effective use of a spell-checker, recognising where it may not be sufficient or appropriate

Modern technology is affecting the use of standard spelling. This is partly because spell-checking programmes may be used as the source of correct spelling, rather than the individual's own knowledge. Obvious limitations of this tool are the problem of homonyms and the differences between American and British English spelling – such as the use of '–ize', rather than '–ise'. The status of spelling is also affected, because the conventions of electronic communication (emails and chatrooms) do not emphasise the importance of correct spelling or punctuation; the priority is to convey the message as swiftly as possible.

The study of morphology can offer pupils some useful spelling strategies (rather than rules).

Deleting the prefix

Many common prefixes have a regular spelling. All prefixes have a single consonant, but are often misspelled as double, for example. Ambrose Bierce (2003) plays on the confusion between the prefix 'mis-' and the word 'miss' in this definition:

> *Misfortune, n. The type of fortune that never misses*

Deleting the prefix from the root can reveal some incorrect doubling of consonants.

* dissappoint	dis– * sappoint	* diss– appoint
* proffessional	pro– * ffessional	* prof– fessional

However, there are always complications. Why is there a double 'ff' combination in the word 'difference'? The reasons for this can be explained by looking at reasons for language change in pronunciation, which gradually affects spelling.

Consonant assimilation occurs to make some combinations of consonants easier to pronounce. The spelling of some prefixes has changed to reflect the easier pronunciation of some combinations of sounds. (This was probably a spelling mistake originally, but is now the standard spelling.) It would be tricky to pronounce the combination of sounds in the word

> * dis-ference

The easier pronunciation of 'dif-ference' is now seen in its modern spelling. Other prefixes which have undergone consonant assimilation are:

ad–	to	ac–	ac–commodation
en–	to	em–	em–power
con–	to	com–/col–	com–memorate/col–lective
in–	to	im–/ir–/il–	im–possible/ir–relevant/il–legitimate

Deleting the suffix

The spelling of suffixes is more regular. Deleting the suffix provides a useful check for spelling.

This suffix is often confused with the related word 'full', causing such spelling mistakes as:

> * success–full
> * wonder–full

The suffix $\boxed{-ly}$ is also misspelled. If the suffix is deleted, the correct spelling shows the word formation:

> * beautifuly   * beautifu–$\boxed{ly}$ $\boxed{beauti}$–$\boxed{ful}$–$\boxed{ly}$
>
> * immediatley   * immediat–*ley $\boxed{immediate}$ –$\boxed{ly}$

NB You can always be caught out, as this common example shows:

> * truely   true + ly   tru –ly

Some words with the suffix $\boxed{-able}$ have altered the spelling to $\boxed{-ible}$. These changes are often – but not always! – after roots ending in 's' or 'se':

	–able	–		ible
teach	teachable	but	response	respons$\boxed{ible}$
pass	passable	but	?	poss$\boxed{ible}$
play	playable	but	reprehend	reprehens$\boxed{ible}$

In the case of such irregular spellings, it is appropriate for pupils to use a spell-checker. For example, a common exception to the 'rule' offered above is:

> use useable   not * usible   or * usable

Unlike '–able', other suffixes $\boxed{-age}$, $\boxed{-ity}$ beginning in a vowel tend to drop the 'e' ending in roots. For example:

> * useage becomes usage
> * probeity becomes probity

The suffix $\boxed{-ent}$ is often spelt '–ant'. For example, I am never sure how to spell words such as:

　　　*independant　　　independent

This is because the unstressed syllable is pronounced with a schwa sound and could be represented by either 'a' or 'e'.

Changes in the pronunciation of English over time also involve vowel **elision** – the omission of vowel sounds. Some changes in pronunciation have passed into standard spellings. In these cases, it is the root of the word that undergoes assimilation:

　　　*pronounce + –iation　　　pronunci[ation]

　　　*terror + –ible　　　terr[ible]

　　　*horrid + –ible　　　horr[ible]

The omission of vowel sounds in spoken language causes some incorrect spellings:

　　　*comftable　　　*comft –able　　　[comfort] – [able]

　　　*buisness　　　*buis –ness　　　[busi] –[ness]

These common misspellings are less easy to explain by the rules of morphology:

　　　*choclate　　　borrowed from South American language

　　　*libry　　　?　　　　　　　　　　　　　　　　[libr][–ary]

The next activity uses knowledge of morphology to clarify the correct vs incorrect spellings of the following tricky words.

Activity 3.3

- Which is the correct spelling in each pair of words?
- Use your understanding of roots, prefixes and suffixes to explain why one option is the standard spelling.

aggressive	agressive
despair	dispair
prefferred	preferred
comitted	committed
dissapear	disappear
reccommend	recommend
ocasion	occasion
irresistable	irresistible
irritable	irritible
changeable	changible

realy	really
insistant	insistent
existance	existence
concientious	conscientious

Language in use

I never know whether to use a hyphen or not.
Is it 'word processor' or 'word-processor' or 'wordprocessor'?

Use of hyphens

The use of **hyphens** is an aspect of spelling where an awareness of the processes of language change is useful. New words are often created to match a changing world.

For example, with the advent of steam locomotives, the tracks they ran on needed a name. Initially a compound, e.g.

> *rail way*

would be used as two separate words. As it comes into common use, such compounds tend to go through a process of hyphenisation, e.g.

> *rail–way*

towards becoming a single word, e.g.

> *railway*

Thus the hyphen generally signals that the two words are approaching acceptance as a single word for a single concept. At this stage of the process of language change, there is usually variation, with the two (or even all three) forms coexisting. Going to a dictionary for the definitive answer is rarely effective, as dictionaries are out of date as soon as they are published! The following words are examples of this 'fuzzy' area of language change.

Activity 3.4

Survey a group of people about the spelling of the following words. Do they see them as two separate words, two words with a hyphen, or a single word?

homework	*spellchecker*
housework	*chatroom*
coursework	*desktop*
wordprocessor	*laptop*

This brings the study of morphology to a close. The next three chapters deal with word classes. Although the most useful way of identifying types of words is by their *role* (the way they operate in language structure), pupils can use their knowledge of suffixes to recognise the *form* of nouns, verbs, adjectives and adverbs.

4

Words, words, words

This chapter moves from morphemes up to the next level of language structure: individual words.

TABLE 4.1 Levels of structure

One or more **morphemes**	combine to form	words.
One or more **words**	combine to form	phrases.
One or more **phrases**	combine to form	clauses.
One or more **clauses**	combine to form	sentences.
One or more **sentences**	combine to form	paragraphs and whole texts.

The ability to label types of words as nouns, verbs and so on is what many people think grammar *is*. Perhaps this is because single words are the most obvious parts of language. But it is essential to recognise words as the first level of syntax. They form the basis for combinations into the succeeding levels of grammatical structure: *phrases*, which can then be combined into *clauses*, in turn forming the basis for various types of *sentence* structure.

However, the fact is that most of the terminology used in the Literacy Strategy refers to types of words, with relatively few terms for the higher levels of phrases, clauses and sentences. The glossary for Key Stages 1 and 2 suggests that all these terms have been introduced in primary school. Brief definitions may enable pupils to label simple textbook examples, but the question for teachers remains: Why is this explicit knowledge useful?

The phrasing of the Framework indicates the aims of grammar study at Key Stages 3 and 4. Pupils should: 'understand and have the terminology to describe the role of word classes'. The emphasis is on *understanding* and the *roles* of different types of words. This may seem a minor point, but it is crucial to the study of word classes. The terminology is not used for 'naming' the words themselves, but to describe the ways they function in language use.

There are three ways of explaining word classes.

- A definition by *meaning* can only identify the most obvious examples.
- Awareness of *form* (morphology) is a useful guide.
- Understanding the *function* of each word class is the essential strategy.

The meaning and form of each word class is mentioned briefly, before exploring the function. Activities use the four principles of *substitution, deletion, insertion* and *transposition* to develop understanding of the ways words operate in the structure of English.

I hope other teachers will share the 'growing feeling that grammar teaching has an unfulfilled potential, particularly if it reflects contemporary English' (NLS, 2004). Wherever possible, activities are based on authentic examples of language in use. The 'potential' of study of word classes is indicated in applications to

- **language variation** – understanding the main differences between standard and non-standard uses of English
- **writing** – the use of appropriate style in more formal contexts
- **reading** – understanding the ways meanings may be implied by choice of vocabulary.

This chapter begins by demonstrating the flexible roles of individual words in English and language users' innate understanding of grammar, before looking at each of the main word classes in detail. It begins with the 'nuts and bolts' – prepositions and conjunctions. Chapter 5 looks at nouns, determiners and pronouns. Chapter 6 looks at the remaining classes of verb, adjective and adverb.

Key words

word class   content vs grammatical   open vs closed   letter string   function

---

Language in use

A word, in a word, is complicated. (Pinker, 1994)

Language is a process of free creation; its laws and principles are fixed, but the manner in which the principles of generation are used is free and infinitely varied. Even the interpretation and use of words involves a process of free creation. (Noam Chomsky, 1970)

Word classes

The ability to name the different parts of speech – or type of word – is straightforward in a sense, as nearly all the words in English can be classified into eight **word classes**. Before exploring each one in detail, there is a useful, initial distinction. The word classes can be grouped as follows:

content/open classes	*grammatical/closed classes*
noun	*pronoun*
verb	*preposition*
adjective	*determiner*
adverb	*conjunction*

The first group contains the types of words that convey meaning in obvious ways, hence **content** word classes. In the second group, the words do not convey meanings in this obvious way, but function as the 'nuts and bolts' – or **grammatical** word classes.

A further distinction between the two groups is their size and capacity for change. There is a limited and stable number of pronouns or prepositions, but nouns or verbs run to tens of thousands, with new additions to the store, as well as losses. The terms **open** and **closed** refer to this aspect.

The terms for these word classes are mostly familiar, so why does Pinker say that a word is 'complicated' and why does the whole business of identifying nouns and verbs often cause so much anxiety? This is because words cannot be pinned down into a fixed class. A recognisable **letter string**, such as 'light' (see Introduction page 10) can **function** as either a noun, verb, adjective or adverb. The potential of language for creativity and variation, as noted by Chomsky, is a double-edged sword: a flexible resource for users, but challenging for those looking for quick answers. However, the principles for creating new forms of language are not only 'fixed', but understood intuitively.

The next section demonstrates how pupils can use their intuitive understanding of the roles of word classes – the ways that they can use the same letter string for different functions. The concepts of form and function will be used to explain each class of word. Activities draw on pupils' explicit knowledge of morphology – roots, prefixes and suffixes – to analyse the form of different word classes.

Key words

verb   form

Language in use

A He <u>hitted</u> me. He's a puncher he is.
There I <u>unflatted</u> it.
I <u>hammed</u> those all by myself.

B I'm <u>souping</u>.
I'm <u>darking</u> the sky.
<u>Put</u> me that broom.
Let's get <u>brooming</u>.

C I'm <u>swimming</u> my duck.
These flowers are <u>sneezing</u> me.
I can't <u>die</u> this spider.
I'm going to <u>fall</u> this on her.

D How do you <u>sharp</u> this?
<u>Full</u> this up.
You have to <u>scale</u> it.
I'm going to <u>earth</u> this.
Why didn't you <u>jam</u> my bread?

> **E** I <u>hate</u> you and I'll never <u>unhate</u> you or nothing.
> How did you <u>unsqueezed</u> it?

'Virtuous errors'

These are examples of the language use of children aged 3–4 years (Peccei, 1994). Young children use their limited repertoire of words in creative ways to express themselves. Chomsky uses the term 'virtuous errors' for examples of child language that depart from standard, adult language but demonstrate an intuitive grasp of underlying rules of grammar. A parrot, or a computer, can *imitate* words, but children effortlessly *create* new, meaningful forms of language.

The clearest examples of a child's intuitive grammar occur in their creative use of **verbs**. Although the root may not be a conventional verb, they use standard verb **forms** to express a variety of functions.

Activity 4.1

Explain how the verbs underlined in the box above show a child's intuitive grasp of grammar.
- What suffixes and prefixes does the child use? (form)
- What meanings do these express? (function)
- What is unusual about the child's use of these roots for verbs?
  - 'soup', 'broom', 'scale', 'earth', 'jam', 'hammer'
  - 'dark', 'sharp', 'full', 'flat'
- Rephrase the examples in Group C to show the standard use of these verbs:
  - 'swim', 'sneeze', 'die', 'fall'

Changing the role of words

This creative ability goes 'underground' while children learn standard forms of language. It re-emerges in the innovative language of literature and advertising.

> He *unseam'd him from the nave to the chaps.* (Macbeth, *Act I, scene ii*)
> '*You've been Tangoed!' (advert for soft drink)*

In both these examples, we see words that were originally nouns – 'seam' and 'Tango' – used as verbs. Pupils can demonstrate this ability to change word class in activities such as Activity 4.2. This shows that many words, or 'letter strings', can be used for various functions. Words normally used as nouns can change their form to function as verbs.

Activity 4.2

- Name things you can see or hear in the classroom. These words are nouns.
- Challenge another student to use the word as a verb.

For example:

wall	*they <u>were walling</u> us in.*
OHP	*our teacher <u>OHPed</u> us for an hour.*

Application to language variation and change

This process of changing nouns to verbs occurs in language change, with many examples now accepted as standard English: '*chair* a meeting'. In contemporary language use, this type of change to word class is often associated with business jargon, or Americanisms, and thus disliked:

> Can you <u>action</u> this?
> Let's <u>flag</u> it up.

Similar activities can explore other types of words that can be used as verbs:

adjective: big	*verb: <u>Big</u> me up!*
preposition: up	*verb: She <u>upped</u> and left.*

There is no accepted term for these changes in the role of words, but the term 'nominalisation' (see p.64) refers to changes from verb to noun. Before looking at the content word classes – noun, verb, adjective and adverb – the following sections deal with two grammatical word classes: prepositions and conjunctions.

Grammatical word classes

Language in use

Think of words as instruments characterized by their use, and then think of the use of a hammer, the use of a chisel, the use of a square, of a glue pot, and of the glue.

(*Wittgenstein*, The Blue Book)

The study of word classes often begins with nouns, verbs, adjectives and adverbs, as the content words have the more obvious uses of 'hammers' and 'chisels'. In order to understand their roles, however, it is helpful to recognise the 'glue' in the structure of English. These are the grammatical word classes, used in full sentences, but omitted in abbreviated forms, such as notices and headlines. The days of sending telegrams are gone, but such condensed messages illustrate language with only content words. Pupils will intuitively fill in the gaps with grammatical words to make the meaning precise.

Activity 4.3

- What do you understand by the following message?
- What words might you add to make it clearer?

> *Friends fly New York find bargains top designer stores clothes too expensive buy only jeans return home.*

The final sections in this chapter deal with two grammatical word classes – conjunctions and prepositions.

Conjunctions

Key words

connective   conjunction   co-ordinating conjunction   subordinating conjunction

Some of the grammatical words added in the previous activity function as links. The term **connective** is used in the Framework as an overall term for a variety of ways of linking structures:

Conjunction	*The clothes were too expensive, so they only bought a pair of jeans.*
Adverb	*They bought a pair of jeans, before returning home.*
Non-finite verb	*Disappointed by the trip, they returned home.*

This section provides a brief introduction to the word class of **conjunctions**. (See Chapter 10 for further exploration of sentence structure.)

Types of conjunction

The term conjunction indicates the function of this word class – to join parts of the structure together. The most frequently used conjunction is the word 'and'. It is used to express a simple sequence of items or events. It also the first tool that children acquire for creating longer stretches of language. For these reasons, the use of 'and' has an impact on style.

Co-ordinating conjunctions

The distinction between **co-ordinating** and **subordinating conjunctions** helps to explain some stylistic differences. There are only four co-ordinating conjunctions:

and, but, so, or

Their function is to link parts in a straightforward way: expressing addition, opposition, consequences or alternatives. The resulting structure can be compared to a linear string of links. The television comedy *Little Britain* creates the voice of an inarticulate teenager, Vicky Pollard, by the repeated use of these simple conjunctions:

> *Yeah, but no, but so, anyway . . .*

Activity 4.4

- Identify the conjunctions used in the following extract from a narrative.
- What is the effect of this style?

> I said, 'Who killed him?' and he said, 'I don't know who killed him but he's dead all right,' and it was dark and there was water standing in the street and no lights and windows broke and boats all up in the town and trees blown down and everything all blown and I got a skiff and went out and found my boat where I had her inside Mango Bay and she was all right only she was full of water.
>
> (Hemingway, After the Storm)

Application to style and formality

Pupils should be able to recognise repeated use of co-ordinating conjunctions as a marker of a simple – even childlike – style. One aim for their own writing skills, however, is to develop a repertoire of conjunctions to form a variety of sentence structures. The repeated use of 'and', 'but' and 'so' is often an indication of a lower level of achievement. (See Chapter 10 on compound sentences.)

Subordinating conjunctions

Subordinating conjunctions combine structures in a more complex way. This can be compared to a three-dimensional model, with structures 'embedded' within the sentence.

> <u>Unless</u> *dinner money is paid on Monday, pupils will not be able to have a school meal, as they must be ordered in advance.*

This word class is closed, so it is possible to list all conjunctions. Some common subordinating conjunctions are

> *because, as, since, so, although, unless, if, when, which, while*

These conjunctions express various relationships with the main clause: reasons, consequences, examples, exceptions, etc. (See Chapter 10 on sentence structure.)

A rule that is often quoted is: 'You should never start a sentence with a conjunction.' This, like most rules, is over-simple. It only refers to the three co-ordinating conjunctions, 'and', 'but', 'or'. Sentences can – and often do – begin with subordinating conjunctions: 'although', 'unless', etc. And yet there are many examples of sentences beginning with 'and'! Departing from this norm emphasises it as a stylistic device. Pupils should be aware that the normal role of co-ordinating conjunctions is to link parts of structure. These stylistic issues are discussed further in Chapter 10 (on sentence structure) and in Chapter 13 (on discourse).

TABLE 4.2 Conjunctions summary

Function	Co-ordinating conjunctions normally occur as links between parts of the sentence. Subordinating conjunctions occur at the beginning of a clause and can be placed at the beginning of a sentence.
Form	Conjunctions do not change their form.
Meaning	Conjunctions express various relationships between parts of the sentence: addition, opposition, cause, effect, etc.

Prepositions

The examples below show a few differences between standard and non-standard uses of prepositions. Native speakers of English, however, intuitively use prepositions accurately. In addition, prepositions are a closed word class, with a finite number of members, so this section will be relatively brief. The ability to recognise prepositions will be used in Chapter 7 in the study of noun and adverbial phrases.

Key words
preposition   phrasal verb

Language in use
Get off of it.
You shouldn't of done it.
This is something I will not put up with.
Ending a sentence with a preposition is something up with which I will not put.
I parked the van in back of the house.
I can't come out while ten o'clock.

Prepositions with nouns

The term **preposition** itself indicates the function of this word class: their position is commonly before ('pre–') nouns. They can convey meanings such as position in time and space.

Substitution test

Pupils can use the substitution test to build on their knowledge of familiar prepositions.

Activity 4.5

- What words can replace these prepositions?

  On   the window

  At   three o'clock

       Sunday

       the afternoon

Prepositions with verbs

Although prepositions often occur before nouns, they can also function after verbs. This use is common in English, creating a variety of **phrasal verbs** with complex shades of meaning. These are tricky for learners of English, but are used effortlessly by native speakers. Their use tends to be informal, as there is often a more formal alternative. For example:

I can't   *put up with*   *noise.*

I can't   *tolerate*   *noise.*

Activity 4. 6

- Note the various prepositions that can follow the verb 'take', conveying different meanings.

  Take

  The plane took off.

  She took off her teacher.

  Don't take on too much work.

  I can't take in so much information.

  These books take up so much space.

  I'm going to take up karate.

- Create as many different phrasal verbs as possible by adding a different preposition to verbs, such as 'give' and 'make'.

- Use each one in a sentence to make the meaning clear.

Applications to standard English

Prepositions are generally used without problem, but there is sometimes confusion in the use of 'of' and 'off'. The examples at the beginning of the section (page 51) showed some common errors.

'Get off of it.'

The colloquial use of both prepositions is considered non-standard, so should be avoided in formal situations.

'You shouldn't of done it.'

A much stronger warning is needed in errors such as this. It is becoming so common that its use was noted in a letter from Central Trains:

> *You should of complained to the official present on the train.*

This type of error is influenced by spoken language, where the abbreviated form of 'have' may sound like 'of'. However, its use in written language is highly stigmatised, as it is clearly ungrammatical. A substitution test demonstrates that prepositions cannot function in this role.

> *You   should   <u>of</u>   come.*
> ** on*
> ** in*
> ** with*

'This is something I will not put up with.'

The third example is less clear-cut. Prescriptive grammars used to prohibit the use of prepositions at the end of sentences. This view is mocked in the 'correct' version:

> *Ending a sentence with a preposition is something up with which I will not put.*

In contemporary use, prepositions often occur at the end of sentences:

> *I need more money to live <u>on</u>.*
> *I got the job I applied <u>for</u>.*
> *Who did you go out <u>with</u>?*
> *Noise is something I can't put <u>up with</u>.*

The effort to avoid this leads to rather clumsy, hyper-formal constructions:

> *I need more money on which to live.*
> *I got the job for which I applied.*
> *Out with whom did you go?*
> *Noise is something up with which I cannot put.*

This is one example of changing attitudes to grammar – if a structure is effective in conveying meaning, then it is acceptable in use.

'I parked the van in back of the house.'

There is some variation between standard US English and standard British English. US English can use 'in back of' as the opposite of 'in front of', showing the tendency for US English to retain regular patterns – as an earlier example of the verb 'gotten' vs 'got'.

'I can't come out while ten o'clock.'

In some northern dialects of English, the preposition 'while' is used in place of until. This can cause ambiguity:

> *Vehicles must wait <u>until</u> the barrier is raised.*
> *Vehicles must wait <u>while</u> the barrier is raised.*

TABLE 4.3 Prepositions summary

Function	occur before nouns, after verbs, or *alone as adverbs*
Form	simple morphemes, with no addition of suffixes
Meaning	position in time or space, possession, accompaniment, etc. In phrasal verbs, they convey a variety of meanings

The two remaining grammatical word classes – determiners and pronouns – are explored in Chapter 5, as they always function with nouns.

5

Nouns and pronouns

Nouns have a significant role in any language. There are hundreds of thousands of words in English and the majority of these are nouns. The first words a child speaks are mainly nouns for the important people and things in their world. Attempts to communicate with chimpanzees use pictures to represent objects. Perhaps the origins of language began with nouns? The need to identify new phenomena accounts for a large part of language change: most of the entries in any dictionary of new words are nouns, with fewer additions to verbs and adjectives.

Clearly the need to name our world of experience is a vital function of language. But the simple definition – 'a noun is a naming word' – is not a reliable way of identifying all nouns. It works for obvious, textbook examples – 'house', 'dog', 'tree' – where there is immediate agreement. As soon as there is doubt over more tricky examples, the debate has nowhere to go. If you ask pupils to identify the 'naming words' in this paragraph, they might reasonably pick out 'name', 'language', 'word', 'textbook', 'agreement'. Some of these words are nouns, but 'name' is definitely not, and 'textbook' is debatable. Other nouns may be overlooked: 'way', 'world', 'function'. How can teachers explain that 'name' is not a naming word; that 'textbook' may be the name of something, but is used in a different way here; and that 'function' is a noun, even if it doesn't seem to name anything?

The approach to grammar throughout the book is to concentrate on the *structure* of language. Words operate in this structure in different ways. The term 'noun' is not so much a label for a type of word, but for the *role* – or *function* – it plays in a particular sentence. The four key principles of substitution, insertion, deletion and transposition can demonstrate the function of any word class in a clear, straightforward way.

Activities use these tests to develop pupils' understanding of the role of nouns and the related grammatical classes: determiner and pronoun. The examples used – of authentic language – are often creative and unusual, defying quick answers. But this teaching approach is based on the belief that the best way to explore grammar is by asking questions. Equipped with these skills, teachers and pupils can resolve any doubts in a systematic way.

The ability to identify different types of noun – common vs proper, mass vs count, concrete vs abstract – is rarely explicitly tested, but it has useful applications.

It can explain some differences between standard and non-standard forms of English, as well as levels of formality and implied meanings. The first section begins with the 'nuts and bolts' of English structure – determiners.

Key words
determiner   article   demonstrative   possessive   definite article

Language in use
Train delay funeral anguish. *Climbers trapped on mountain.* *Entry without permit forbidden.* *Put cup on table.*

Determiners

These 'little' grammatical words are used all the time, but hardly noticed. Because they do not convey meaning in an obvious way, they can be omitted, leaving the nouns and verbs to carry the message. The first activity uses such abbreviated forms of language to draw attention to this 'invisible' word class.

Activity 5.1

- Which word is used most often in English spoken and written language?
- Where might you read, or hear, these four examples?
  - *Train delay funeral anguish.*
  - *Climbers trapped on mountain.*
  - *Entry without permit forbidden.*
  - *Put cup on table.*
- Which words have been omitted in these abbreviated structures?
- Why might their role be thought of as 'glue' or 'nuts and bolts'?

What is a determiner?

The words omitted from Activity 5.1 are determiners. The immediate problem with the term **determiner** for this word class is its unfamiliarity. It may seem an unnecessary complication to introduce new terminology, when **article** is already familiar as a label for the two common words 'a' and 'the'. But many other words can operate in this role. It is useful to have one overall term to describe this word class, before learning the labels for each individual word: '**possessive** pronoun', '**demonstrative** article', etc.

Determiners can be explained by their *meaning*: they express concepts such as number and quantity. The *form* of determiners is relatively constant: they rarely change, by the addition of suffixes or prefixes. The most useful definition is the way they *function*: determiners are words that come before nouns. The function can be explored by using the key tests.

Substitution test

The substitution test can be used to show which other words share the same role as the familiar determiners 'a' and 'the'.

Activity 5.2

- Use the substitution test to see which other words can replace 'a' and 'the'.

| Put | <u>a</u> | cup on | <u>the</u> | table. |
| Put | _ | cups on | _ | tables. |

Applications to style and levels of formality

Year 8: understand the main differences between standard English and dialectal variations

The Framework for Key Stages 1 and 2 includes terminology for three subclasses of determiner: article, demonstrative and possessive. These terms can be used to explain some common differences between standard and non-standard – or dialectal – uses of English.

The use of the **definite article** 'the' accounts for one difference: in some dialects of spoken English, it is omitted or abbreviated:

> *Put (t) cup on (t) table.*

The term demonstrative includes the words 'this', 'that', 'these', 'those'. This term can highlight a non-standard use of determiner:

> *Give me * <u>them</u> books.*
> *Give me <u>those</u> books.*

Possessive, as the name suggests, refers to words such as 'my', 'your', 'her', 'his', 'its'. These can be replaced by any name, such as 'Alison's', 'Fred's', etc. This causes a common mistake in the use of the apostrophe. Although expressing 'possession', the determiners have no apostrophe. This is clearly not possible for most – '* hi's' – but the distinction between 'its' and 'it's' is often confused.

> *The dog was chasing * it's tail.*
> *The dog was chasing its tail.*

NB Words such as 'my', 'our', 'his', 'her' may seem to have more in common with 'pronouns', as they are related to words such as 'I', 'we', 'he', 'she'. They belong to the word class of determiner, however, because they perform the same role in sentence structures. A later section explores the different role of pronouns (see page 67).

Insertion and deletion tests

The examples so far have shown a straightforward use of determiners – occurring immediately before a noun. But often the structure is more complex, including other types of words before a noun. The tests of insertion and deletion can be used to distinguish determiners from adjectives and nouns. (See Chapter 6 on adjectives and Chapter 7 on noun phrases.)

Other types of words can be inserted before nouns to provide additional information:

> Put some <u>coffee</u> cups on those <u>side</u> tables.
> The <u>high-speed</u> train hit a <u>parked</u> car.

Determiners are generally essential to the grammatical structure; they cannot be deleted in most written texts. Other types of words can be deleted, as the following activity shows.

Activity 5.3

- Are these words determiners: 'side', 'coffee', 'special', 'tea', 'main'?
- Does the structure remain intact if you remove these words from the following sentences?
  - *Put some coffee cups on those side tables.*
  - *Leave my special tea cup on this main table.*

TABLE 5.1 Determiners summary

Function	always occur before nouns – cannot be deleted
Form	often single morphemes with no addition of suffixes or prefixes
Meaning	can express meanings such as number or quantity

The next section moves from determiners to nouns, as the two classes operate together in English structures.

Identifying types of nouns

This section uses pupils' intuitive awareness of language use to develop an explicit understanding of the terms for different types of nouns. It also introduces the concept of 'nominalisation', included in the Framework for Key Stages 3 and 4. This knowledge can be applied to understanding of degrees of formality and the ways meanings are implied in texts.

Key words

noun: proper/common, abstract/concrete,
mass/count, nominalisation

Language in use

What is a must?
Stop being such a know-it-all.
The unbearable lightness of being.

What is a noun?

The most familiar definition is based on the *meaning* this class of word conveys, i.e. 'a noun is a naming word'. But this is not the most useful or reliable way of understanding what a **noun** is. Thinking about meaning may not help pupils to identify 'must', 'know-it-all' or 'being' as nouns in the examples above. (The first example was a question referring to a poster, 'Windsor Castle is a Must'; the third is the title of a book.) However, the notion of naming words can be used in a preliminary activity to collect some examples of 'classic' nouns. Pupils may have been told what some of their first words were. These are often nouns, used to name – or ask for – important people and things in their world, such as:

> *mummy, daddy, baby, ball, dog, cat, juice, milk, biscuit, shoe, car*

Even with such apparently straightforward examples of nouns, some caution is needed. As Chapter 4 showed, it is not possible to identify the class of a word in isolation. Many words normally encountered as nouns can be used in different ways. In order to identify the class, the word must be seen in context. For example, the word 'baby' may be used as a verb:

> *Don't baby me.*

Thus, the fundamental definition of any word class is based on its *function*. Words are classified as nouns because they operate in similar ways in the structure of language. The four tests of substitution, insertion, deletion and transposition show how nouns are used in English structure.

Substitution test

Pupils can use their store of known nouns in substitution tests to see whether an unfamiliar word is a noun. If you can replace a word with a noun, this suggests that those words share the role of a noun. The structure should remain grammatical, even though the sense might be strange. For example:

I want more ticky.	*Give the wug to me.*	*We need your compliance.*
juice	*ball*	*car*
milk	*mummy*	*biscuit*

Activity 5.4

Use the substitution test to identify the nouns in the following.

What is a must?

Stop being such a know-it-all.

The Unbearable Lightness of Being.

NB You might also use inventive texts, such as 'The Jabberwocky' by Lewis Carroll, for this activity.

Form

Another way of identifying nouns is based on their *form*. Nouns can change their form to indicate singular or plural. Another change in form indicates possession. Pupils can use their knowledge of morphology to identify the types of suffix that can be added to nouns. Awareness of the close connection between determiners and nouns can be consolidated in such activities.

Activity 5.5

The underlined words in the following text are nouns.

- How can you tell a noun is plural? (form)
- How do nouns show that something belongs to them? (form)
- What words often come before a noun? (function)

> *What is the difference between an <u>alligator</u> and a <u>crocodile</u>? Well, first of all the <u>alligator</u> has a broad <u>snout</u> and all of its <u>teeth</u> in the upper <u>jaw</u> overlap those in the lower <u>jaw</u>. An <u>alligator</u> is slightly bigger than a <u>crocodile</u>, and the <u>crocodile's</u> <u>snout</u> is bigger, and narrower. You can also see a <u>crocodile's</u> enlarged, lower <u>teeth</u> even when its <u>mouth</u> is closed.*
>
> *Male <u>alligators</u> are called <u>bulls</u>. The <u>bull</u> is usually much larger than the female <u>alligator</u>. The male <u>alligator</u> will roar very loudly to call a <u>mate</u> and to scare other <u>bulls</u> away. Female <u>alligators</u> will lay their <u>eggs</u> in a <u>nest</u>.*
>
> *(www.kidscape.com)*

Insertion and deletion tests

This knowledge of form can be used to identify nouns, by using the tests of insertion or deletion.

Activity 5.6

- Identify the nouns in the following quotation:

    Workers of the world unite. You have nothing to lose but your chains.

- Can you add, or remove, the suffix '–s' to change the word from singular to plural?
- If you are not sure, try the substitution test, or your awareness of determiners.

These aspects of form and function can be used to explain subclasses of noun:

common	*vs*	*proper*
concrete	*vs*	*abstract*
countable	*vs*	*mass*

Common vs proper nouns

One important distinction is between **common** and **proper nouns**. This knowledge can be applied to the use of capital letters and to explore aspects of language variation and change.

Language in use

Literature or literature?
One God or many gods?
The internet or the Internet?
Save now with abbey.
e e cummings
We've got a lot of Hayleys in Year 9.

Proper nouns are often defined by their *meaning*: names of people, places and organisations. They are distinguished in writing by the use of a capital letter, but the examples above show some variation. The same letter string can be used as a proper or common noun: 'literature' and 'Literature'. The next activity uses the insertion test to explore some differences in the *form* and *function* of proper vs common nouns.

Activity 5.7

- Compile a list of proper nouns – names for specific people, places, organisations, etc. that are normally written with a capital letter.
- Make a second list of common nouns – more general terms for people, places, things, etc.

For example,

Hayley	*teenager*
Austria	*country*
December	*winter*
Coronation Street	*park*
Abbey National	*bank*

- Can you add '–s' to form a plural? (form)
- Can you insert determiners like 'a', 'an', 'the' before the word? (function)

Applications to language variation and change

The meaning, form and function of proper vs common nouns can be used to explain the distinction between:

Literature	*literature*
God	*god*
Internet	*internet*
Abbey	*abbey*
E. E. Cummings	*e e cummings*
Hayley	*Hayleys*

Capital letters are used in English to confer a sense of respect and uniqueness, when referring to God or Literature. The lower case initial letter suggests a more general reference. The poet e e cummings did not use this distinction in his poetry, or for his own name. This trend can be seen in contemporary brand names, perhaps appearing more modern and unassuming. It is also common in language use in emails and text messages, where capital letters are often omitted for names or the pronoun 'I'. It is important for pupils to use the appropriate style when writing in more formal situations.

Even when names of individual people or organisations are represented with a lower-case initial letter, they still function like proper nouns – they do not take a plural form or follow a determiner.

> * *I'm banking with the barclay.*

When names are used as common nouns – taking a determiner or a plural suffix – this structure is marked as unusual:

Are you the e e cummings?
We've got a lot of Hayleys in Year 9.

The status of the relatively new word 'internet' is interesting. My computer signals a mistake if I do not use a capital letter, but lower case is often used in the media, for example. Although it rarely occurs in a plural form, it is usually preceded by the definite article. Perhaps it depends on the attitude of the writer: 'the Internet' is special and unique in the eyes of Microsoft, but on a par with 'the library' for journalists and teachers?

Count vs mass nouns

Language in use		
five items or less	*or*	*five items or fewer*
My sister has brown hairs.	*or*	*My sister has brown hair.*
I don't like fishes.	*or*	*I don't like fish.*

The distinction between these subclasses of nouns can be used to explain some differences between standard and non-standard English, such as the examples above.

One way of explaining the difference between **count** and **mass nouns** is based on *meaning*. Count nouns, as the name suggests, are said to refer to things that can be counted. Mass nouns are sometimes called 'uncountable', as they refer to entities regarded as a single unit. This distinction is not always a matter of common sense. Try dividing the following words into those that can be counted and those that cannot:

money, cash, wage, coin, loaf, bread, fish, hair

A definition based on meaning would include 'money' and 'cash' as things that can be counted, yet they do not belong to the class of count nouns.

Insertion test

A more reliable definition is based on *form*. Count nouns can take a plural form; mass nouns cannot. It is now a straightforward task to identify the mass and count nouns, using the insertion test.

Activity 5.8

Classify these nouns as mass or count nouns.

Which nouns can take a plural form – can add the '–s' suffix? (form)

money, cash, wage, coin, loaf, bread, fish, hair

Applications to standard and non-standard English

Mass and count nouns can also be distinguished by the ways they *function* in relation to other words. The previous activities showed that common nouns are generally preceded by determiners, such as 'the' and 'a'. There are some differences in the determiners used before mass and count nouns.

> *How <u>much</u> cash is there?*   *How <u>many</u> coins are there?*
> *There is <u>less</u> cash now.*   *There are <u>fewer</u> coins now.*

Language users rarely confuse 'much' and 'many', but the distinction between 'less' and 'fewer' is disappearing in contemporary English. The following examples are both considered non-standard:

> *There is too much exams these days.*
> *School pupils will take less exams in the revised curriculum.*

Perhaps only the first example struck you as 'ungrammatical'? The second example is becoming so common in contemporary use that it may soon be accepted as standard. Sir Mike Tomlinson (former Chief Inspector for Education) used the phrase 'less exams' in place of the standard 'fewer exams' in an interview on Radio 4. The few people that noticed phoned in to complain about his 'incorrect' grammar.

Although most people do not 'know or care about' this aspect of grammar, teachers might like to be aware of the changing use and attitudes. Supermarket checkout counters provide evidence of this. It is common to find signs reading

> *9 items or less*

but there is some variation, depending on the company and its location. In 1994, for example, Marks and Spencer used the standard form

> *5 items or fewer*

However, in its stores in Sheffield, it has changed to the more common use of

> *5 items or less*

The standard version is still used in the south of England, though. We can see that the standard form retains its prestige, but the distinction is rarely observed, except in the most formal situations.

Concrete vs abstract nouns

In this distinction, the differences in *meaning* are fundamental. **Abstract nouns** refer to qualities or states, while **concrete nouns** refer to material entities that can be perceived by the five senses.

Activity 5.9

Use the meaning definition to identify the abstract and concrete nouns in the following.

> Lord, make me an instrument of your peace.
> Where there is hatred...let me sow love.
> Where there is injury...pardon.
>
> Where there is discord...unity.
> Where there is doubt... faith.
> Where there is error...truth.
> Where there is despair...hope.
> Where there is sadness...joy.
> Where there is darkness...light.

(peace prayer, attributed to St Francis)

Form

Many abstract nouns can be recognised by their morphology. They are often derived from adjectives, verbs and other nouns, using these suffixes:

child + *hood*

scholar + *ship*

free + *dom*

dull + *ness*

classic + *ism*

pedestrian + *isation*

Year 8: identify the key alterations made to a text when it is changed from an informal to a formal text, e.g. nominalisation

Applications to style and levels of formality

The use of abstract nouns is a feature of many formal types of writing. The term **nominalisation** is used to describe the process of using a verb as a noun – generally an abstract noun. This change of word class can happen in three ways.

The noun may be formed by the addition of a suffix:

> You must <u>behave</u>. *(verb)*   Your <u>behaviour</u> is bad. *(noun)*

There may be an internal change to the form of the word:

> I want to <u>choose</u>. *(verb)*   Give me a <u>choice</u>. *(noun)*

The change in word class may not involve any change in the form of the word:

> We need to <u>change</u>. *(verb)*   <u>Change</u> is vital. *(noun)*

This term, 'nominalisation', is used in the Key Stage Framework to identify a common feature of formal writing. For example, verbs in the first sentence are changed to nouns in the second:

> We have _decided_ not to _begin_ _liaising_ with community groups.
> We have taken the _decision_ to defer _implementation_ of _liaison_ with community groups.

An activity such as the following can draw pupils' attention to the use of nominalisation in formal writing.

Activity 5.10

- Underline the verbs in the first and the changes to nouns in the second.
- How does this affect the tone and style?

Extract 1

You must observe the school rules. Make sure you behave and choose suitable clothes to wear so that the school day runs smoothly. We hope that you will achieve good exam results to benefit us all. We will exclude anyone who departs from these standards.

Extract 2

The observation of the school's code of conduct is a requirement for all pupils. The maintenance of orderly behaviour and the choice of appropriate clothing is essential to the smooth running of the school day. It is our hope that the achievement of academic success will be of benefit to all members of the school community. Any departure from our standards will result in exclusion.

Reading for implied meaning

The use of abstract nouns, including those formed by nominalisation, is a feature of more formal styles of writing. However, choice of vocabulary may not simply alter the level of formality, but have more subtle effects on meaning. The linguist Norman Fairclough (2000) suggests that nominalisation implies meanings in persuasive uses of language, such as political texts. He argues that the role of a verb, such as 'exclude', is to refer to a process. For example,

Year 7: infer and deduce meanings using evidence in the text, identifying where and how meanings are implied

> The school will exclude disruptive pupils.

In this structure, information is conveyed about who performs the action, who is affected and when it happens. In contrast, the role of a noun, such 'exclusion', is to refer to a state:

> We maintain a policy of exclusion.

This structure backgrounds details of the process and foregrounds the positive outcome. Fairclough shows that many political documents prefer the use of a noun to a verb. For example,

In the first leaflet produced by the Social Exclusion Unit, the verb *exclude* is used only once, whereas the nominalisation *exclusion* occurs fifteen times.

(Fairclough, 2000)

Although these examples are more appropriate to undergraduate study, they demonstrate how a straightforward 'naming of parts' may be developed into revealing analysis of ways that meanings are implied in texts.

Activity 5.11

- Read this extract from a speech by Tony Blair.
- Identify the use of nominalisation.
- Is there a significant difference if the nouns are changed to verbs?

> In reality, I believe people do want choice, in public services as in other services. But anyway choice isn't an end in itself. It is one important mechanism to ensure that citizens can indeed secure good schools and health services in their communities. And choice matters as much within those institutions as between them: better choice of learning options for each pupil within secondary schools; better choice of access routes into the health service. Choice puts the levers in the hands of parents and patients so that they as citizens and consumers can be a driving force for improvement in their public services. And the choice we support is choice open to all on the basis of their equal status as citizens not on the unequal basis of their wealth.
>
> *(speech on public services, 23 June 2004)*

Use of concrete and abstract nouns

In many texts, there is a mixture of abstract and concrete nouns. Pupils should be able to identify the types of nouns used and then comment on the effect. The following activity uses a political speech, which begins with abstractions but moves to specific instances.

Activity 5.12

- Read this extract from a speech made by President George Bush to the American people after the events of 11 September 2001.
- Identify the progression from abstract nouns to concrete nouns.
- Comment on the effects.

> *Great harm has been done to us. We have suffered great loss. And in our grief and anger we have found our mission and our moment. Freedom and fear are at war. The advance of human freedom – the great achievement of our time, and the great hope of every time – now depends on us. Our nation – this generation – will lift a dark threat of violence from our people and our future. We will rally the world to this cause by our efforts, by our courage. We will not tire, we will not falter, and we will not fail.*
>
> *(Applause.)*
>
> *It is my hope that in the months and years ahead, life will return almost to normal. We'll go back to our lives and routines, and that is good. Even grief recedes with time and grace. But our resolve must not pass. Each of us will remember what happened that day, and to whom it happened. We'll remember the moment the news came – where we were and what we were doing. Some will remember an image of a fire, or a story of rescue. Some will carry memories of a face and a voice gone forever.*
>
> *And I will carry this: It is the police shield of a man named George Howard, who died at the World Trade Center trying to save others. It was given to me by his mom, Arlene, as a proud memorial to her son. This is my reminder of lives that ended, and a task that does not end.*
>
> *(address to the Joint Session of Congress, 20 September 2001)*

TABLE 5.2 Nouns summary

Function	generally preceded by determiners
Form	generally take suffixes '–s', '–'s'. addition of certain suffixes changes other word classes to nouns
Meaning	refer to people, places, institutions, states

The next section on pronouns demonstrates a further way of identifying nouns.

Pronouns

Although native speakers have an intuitive understanding of the role of pronouns, the examples below show some non-standard uses. The ability to identify types of pronoun can be used to explain some differences between standard English and colloquial or dialectal language use. The choice of pronoun can also influence the formality of a text, from impersonal to direct address.

Key words
pronoun: personal, possessive, reflexive, indefinite, interrogative, relative

---

Language in use

What's tha (thou) done?
I'll give thee a clue.
Me and my friend went shopping.
It is I. (or) It is me.
Who did you see? (or) Whom did you see?
I hate football, me.
It was enjoyed by myself.
He did it hisself.
When meeting a lady, one should doff one's cap.
If anyone wishes to apply for the post, they should send their CV.
It was her what did it.
hi there i got your email.

What is a pronoun?

This is straightforward in many ways. As the label suggests, **pronouns** *function* in the place of nouns. The *meaning* is simple to explain: pronouns refer to people (or animals, or things). Like all closed classes, membership of this class is finite. All the pronouns in the English language could be listed, in theory: 'I', 'me', 'mine', 'myself', 'someone', 'who', etc.

The *form* of pronouns is relatively complex, as the glossary of terms suggests. Unlike other languages, modern English no longer has many inflections on nouns, adjectives and verbs. Pronouns still change their form, however, to indicate person, possession and case (whether subject or object of a verb). These different forms are called **personal**, **possessive**, **reflexive**, **indefinite**, **interrogative** and **relative**.

Activities such as the following use pupils' intuitive grasp of the pronoun system. This can be made explicit and the terminology used to explain some differences between standard and non-standard English.

Activity 5.13

- Answer the following questions in as many ways as possible.
- Use a single word each time. (Do not use the name of a person.)

> *Who ate all the pies?*
> _____ *did.*
>
> *Who/What did you see?*
> *I saw* _____ .

> *Whose is this five-pound note?*
>
> *It's _____'s.*
>
> *I earned it (myself).*

Applications to style and levels of formality

The examples at the beginning of the section (see page 67) showed some variations between standard and non-standard uses of English. These differences can be identified and explained, using the terminology for pronouns.

Year 8: understand the main differences between standard English and dialectal variations, e.g. use of pronouns

Personal pronoun: second person

> *What's tha (thou) done?*
> *I'll give thee a clue.*

There have been some changes to the pronoun system of English over time. Many languages still have a distinction between a formal and informal address to another person, e.g: *tu* vs *vous* in French or *du* vs *sie* in German. The older distinction between 'thee' and 'thou' has disappeared from contemporary English, but traces of it remain in some regional dialects. The standard English 'you' is appropriate for formal speaking and writing, with the dialect forms used in colloquial speech, or for dialogue in plays or narratives.

Personal pronoun: first-person forms

> *Me and my friend went shopping.*

Personal pronouns are still inflected to indicate case (subject or object). Although 'Me went shopping' is clearly ungrammatical, the non-standard form is often used in longer subject groups, such as 'Me and my friend' above.

The colloquial use of 'me' has become so common that the standard form 'My friend and I went shopping' may seem over-formal in speech. However, pupils should learn that it is appropriate in formal styles of writing.

This has led to some other changes in pronoun use. Prescriptive grammars, based on Latin, would say that the verb 'to be' is not followed by an object, thus the 'correct' form would be 'It is I' rather than 'It is me'.

Yet the latter structure is used so widely that the former seems hyper-correct. The distinction between 'who' and 'whom' is also rarely observed in contemporary language use: 'Who did you see?' is such a common structure that may be considered standard use, with 'Whom did you see?' only used in the most formal types of writing.

Reflexive pronouns

Reflexive pronouns are used with certain verbs to refer back to the subject:

I washed/enjoyed myself.

They can also be used at the end of the structure for emphasis:

I enjoy football, myself.

The non-standard variation uses the personal pronoun instead:

I hate football, me.

The reverse – also non-standard – happens in attempts to sound formal:

It was enjoyed by myself.

The dialect forms of reflexive pronouns are interesting, as an aspect of language change:

He did it hisself.
They did it theirselves.

Although regarded as non-standard, they actually follow a regular pattern that may once have been standard.

I	*me*	***my***	*myself*	
you	*you*	***your***	*yourself*	
she	*her*	***her***	*herself*	
he	*him*	***his***	*hisself*	*himself*
we	*us*	***our***	*ourselves*	
they	*them*	***their***	*theirselves*	*themselves*

Impersonal pronouns

The pronoun system of English lacks an accepted way of referring to people in general. The impersonal pronoun 'one' is restricted to the most formal speaking and writing situations.

When meeting a lady, one should doff one's cap.

There is no singular pronoun in the English language that includes both genders. This causes problems of style, if the writer intends a general reference.

If anyone wishes to apply for the post, they should send their CV.

It used to be acceptable to use the pronoun 'he' to refer to both males and females. This is no longer the case, as it is misleadingly exclusive.

If a pupil arrives late, he should report to the office.

Some solutions are clumsy:

> *If a pupil arrives late, <u>he or she</u> should report to the office.*

The shorthand solution is sometimes used:

> *If a pupil arrives late, <u>s/he</u> should report to the office.*

The use of 'they' avoids being gender-specific, but risks the charge of being inconsistent, as it uses a plural term to refer to a singular 'person' or 'anyone'.

> *If anyone arrives late, <u>they</u> should report to the office.*

However, many people accept this use today, as the lesser of two evils.

Relative pronouns

> *It was her what did it.*

The term 'relative pronoun' is used for words that function as connectives between phrases or clauses. (See page 48 on conjunctions and Chapter 10 on sentences.)

> *I met the person*   <u>*who*</u> *wanted to buy my TV.*
> *I met the person*   <u>*whom*</u> *(? who) you recommended.*
> *I bought the TV*   <u>*which*</u> *you recommended.*
> *I bought the TV*   <u>*that*</u> *you recommended.*
> *I bought the TV*   *[ ] you recommended.*
> *I bought the TV*   <u>*what*</u> *you recommended.*

Standard English uses 'who' or 'whom' to refer back to a person and 'which' to refer to a thing. 'That' can be used for either, and can sometimes be omitted in English structure. Colloquial uses of 'what', as a relative pronoun, are considered non-standard, so should not be used in formal situations.

Personal pronouns: use of capital letters

> *hi there i got your email*

Unlike other languages, English distinguishes the first person with a capital letter. We may wonder why reference to self is accorded special status, but it remains the standard form, with some variation in use. Forms of electronic communication often omit capital letters, but pupils should use the standard form for most types of writing.

Applications to style and formality

The choice of pronouns also affects the level of formality. A direct address from 'I', the writer, to 'you', the reader, is appropriate in personal forms of writing.

> **Year 8:** identify the key alterations made to a text when it is changed from an informal to a formal text, e.g. changes from first to third person

More formal texts, such as essays and reports, are conventionally impersonal in tone, so tend to avoid such personal reference. At one time, it was an absolute rule that the first and second person 'I' and 'you' should be avoided in essays and reports. However, this convention is now open to debate. Some people feel that it is both clumsy and misleading to rephrase a personal statement:

> *I think that . . .   vs   It is clear that . . .*

The use of 'we' to mean 'I' is no longer generally accepted:

> *We will examine the choice of vocabulary.*

It is still agreed that the reader should not be addressed directly by 'you' in essays and reports:

> *If you think about it, . . .*

Activity 5.14

- Identify the use of pronouns in the following extract from an essay.
- What changes – to pronouns and vocabulary choice – need to be made to make the style more formal?

> *The views on the side of Robert Kilroy-Silk's article I believe have missed the fact that what he has written was on the whole wrong and insensitive. I believe they are hung up on him getting taken off the BBC and feel his views do not play a major factor in relating to his job title. Maybe you feel he's not been allowed his right as a human being in this society to freedom of speech. I feel that freedom of speech is essential in today's society, but I'm an adamant believer that people of responsibility and power should keep their personal views to themselves, especially if they are not the norm, e.g. controversial. On this occasion I am going to have to side with the BBC.*

Applications to style

Pronouns can be used in place of nouns (or noun phrases) to avoid unnecessary repetition. Sometimes, however, pronoun use can cause ambiguity.

Year 7: recognise and remedy ambiguity in sentences, e.g. unclear use of pronouns

In spoken language, pronouns tend to be used more often, as their reference may be made clear by the context. Pupils should be aware of this difference between spoken and written language. Written language does not provide such contextual clues, so more use of nouns is needed, if the writer wishes the meaning to be explicit. The following activity demonstrates the stylistic effects of pronoun use.

Activity 5.15

- Read the following passage by Danuta Reah. Decide who lost a job, who was late, etc.
- Replace some pronouns – 'he', 'him', 'his' – to make the meaning clear.

> ### Extract 1
>
> *Peter walked down the road with David. He wanted to tell him that he knew he had lost his job, and he knew what it felt like, because he had lost his own job last year. It was his own fault, really, because he was always late, though he wasn't sure if he should point this out in case it annoyed him. He did find it easy to understand because he had always had problems with time-keeping himself, unlike him.*

- Now read the following extract from a mystery novel.
- What effects are created by the use of pronouns – 'she', 'her', 'it'?

> ### Extract 2
>
> *She waited. The fog was heavy, now, damp and slightly smoky in her nostrils. It was now or never. Then she heard the footsteps, coming through the fog. It was here! Where from? Behind her? In front? The echoes moved, confusing her, making her turn sharply, this way, that way. Calm down! she admonished herself. You know what to do. Do it! A stone grated behind her. She spun round, and it was there in front of her.*

TABLE 5.3 Pronouns summary

Function	can replace nouns, or noun phrases
Form	change to show number, possession, case, etc.
Meaning	refer to people, animals or things

Chapter 6 looks at the remaining content classes: verbs, adjectives and adverbs.

Verbs, adjectives and adverbs

The final chapter on word classes explores the role of verbs, adjectives and adverbs. As with all the other word classes, the familiar definition based on meaning is developed by concentrating on the function of each type of word. Activities use the four tests to develop pupils' understanding of the recommended terminology for these word classes. This knowledge is applied to awareness of language variation and change, including differences between standard and non-standard English – degrees of formality. Verbs play more complex roles than other word classes, changing form in several ways to express a variety of meanings. The terminology for classifying types of verbs is extensive and may become daunting. For this reason, it is introduced in stages.

In this chapter, the first section introduces some key terms for describing forms of main verbs. Chapter 8 on verb phrases introduces the distinction between a main and an auxiliary verb, with examples of different verb aspects, moods and voices. The distinction between finite and non-finite verbs is illustrated in Chapter 10 on sentence structure.

Verbs

How can pupils develop their ability to identify verbs in creative uses of language, such as the examples below? Like all word classes, a verb is fundamentally defined by its role, or function, but may also be explained by its meaning and form.

Key words
verb: infinitive, regular, irregular   tense: present, past
person   present participle   past participle

What is a verb?

The familiar definition is based on meaning: 'A **verb** is a doing word.' This may help to identify those verbs that express actions, but many verbs are not obviously 'doing' anything. The examples below (in Activity 6.1) from newspaper reports, might suggest actions, even though 'monster', 'paparazzi' ('papped'), 'trouser' and 'magic' are more familiar as nouns. But, in the fifth example, of 'iffing' and 'butting', the problem is that the person is avoiding doing anything.

Many verbs express *states* rather than actions: 'know', 'belong', 'seem', etc. This is true of the most common verb in English. The verb 'to be' is rarely recognised, if the notion of 'doing word' is used. As it is highly **irregular** – changing its *form* in many ways – it should be learned as a special case.

To be

am	*was*	*been*
is		
are	*were*	*being*

The **infinitive** is the form *to + verb*. The **past participle** is the *verb + ed* for **regular** or *en* for many irregular verbs. The **present participle** is the *verb + ing*.

Substitution test

The most reliable way of identifying verbs is by considering their *function*. At this stage, the substitution test can be introduced. If a word can be substituted by a known verb, this suggests it has the role of verb.

Activity 6.1

- Identify the verbs in the following sentences.
- Which words can be replaced by familiar verbs?

Prince Harry was monstered by paparazzi outside a nightclub.
They papped him.
Chris Eubank trousered over £20,000 for one fight.
It can't magic up greater numbers of specialist teachers.
Stop iffing and butting.

Form

Understanding the form of verbs provides a useful tool. Nouns can change form by the addition of suffixes to show plurals and possession. Verbs also change form to show who and when. The terms for these aspects are **person** and **tense**. The forms of modern English verbs are simple compared to many other languages, which use a different form for each person in many tenses. Pupils' intuitive understanding of changes in form and function of English verbs can be used in activities such as the following.

Activity 6. 2

- Invent a verb, or take an example of a new verb – for example; 'mosh', meaning 'stage-diving', as in 'I am not opposed to moshing.'
- Insert a form of the verb in the following sentences:

  I want _____.

  We always _____.

  Nearly everyone is _____.

  My friend never _____.

  Last Saturday I _____.

- How many different forms did you use?
- What did you add to the root?
- Do you know the term for each form?

Applications to standard and non-standard varieties

Year 9: understand the main differences between standard English and dialectal variations, e.g. subject–verb agreement, formation of past tense

Subject–verb agreement in English is simple compared to other languages, as there is only one change in form. In the simple **present** tense, the third person takes an '–s' suffix, with some variation in Black English vernacular:

He go to the café most days.

New verb forms, used in Activity 6.2, always follow regular structures. However, verbs in common use tend to become irregular. The changes occur in the forms of the **past** tense, with two distinct forms for the simple past and the past participle. For example,

verb	past tense	past participle
go	went	(have) gone
see	saw	(have) seen
do	did	(have) done

Although these complex verb forms are usually used effortlessly by native speakers, there are some differences between standard and non-standard (or dialect) forms of English, such as:

I done it.
I seen it.

In these examples, the **past participle** has been used instead of the simple past form. The reverse happens in some non-standard uses of verbs:

Have you took my pen?
I've wrote the essay.

This variation occurs with a group of verbs that share similar forms:

present	past	past participle
write	wrote	written
take	took	taken
give	gave	given
drive	drove	driven
eat	ate	eaten
show	showed	shown
get	got	gotten

NB The verb 'to get' is of particular interest, as it indicates that the language may be changing in this respect. There is variation between standard American English and standard British English:

> *I have gotten.*   vs   *I have got.*

Although standard English no longer uses the '–en' suffix for the past participle of this particular verb, all the others in the group follow the '–en' pattern.

The non-standard forms are becoming common in language use – the Google search engine reveals more than 26,000 'hits' for the phrase 'I have wrote' alone. However, pupils should be aware of the difference between these standard and non-standard forms, so that they can use standard English in formal situations. The examples in Activity 6.3, for example, were taken from the internet.

Activity 6.3

- Identify the verb forms used in the following examples.
- Change to the standard form, where necessary.
- What do these examples (all taken from the internet) show about language change and variation?

> 1 *You will later read this short passage I have wrote.*
>
> 2 *How many times have you wrote a letter to the mag?*
>
> 3 *Take a look at what he has wrote.*
>
> 4 *Mr Hosein Derakhshan has wrote that Sina has been released from prison, after 22 days.*
>
> 5 *All of my employees that have drove it say the same thing.*
>
> 6 *Do you know a friend that has drove while intoxicated in the past month?*
>
> 7 *What has drove me to seek answers is that I had seen a dark-haired Jesus picture.*
>
> 8 *I have gave this long and hard consideration but I'm now 23 years old and I know its very late to decide that I want to become a doctor.*
>
> 9 *I have gave them my information, credit card, etc. and it has been long over the 48 hours that they say I need to wait.*
>
> 10 *God Has Gave Me My Assignment.*

11 *Zhang Yimou's historical kung fu epic* House of Flying Daggers *had took 110 million yuan (nearly 13 million US dollars).*

12 *'Angels Wings Have Took You.'*

13 *'Words I Might Have Ate' (Green Day lyrics)*

14 *If it has been a few weeks since he has ate, then you can do this now.*

15 *A man may fish with the worm that hath eat of a king, and cat of the fish that hath fed of that worm.*

16 *Blessed be ye of Jehovah, that ye have showed this kindness unto your lord.*

17 *I have showed thee new things from this time, even hidden things, which thou hast not known.*

18 *The United States has showed its real face.*

19 *Have you showed this contract to the collection agency?*

20 *Should BBC have showed the Jerry Springer opera?*

Forming nouns and adjectives from verbs

One way of identifying verbs is by their form: the suffixes '–ing', '–ed'. However, this is not always a reliable way of identifying verbs. Many adjectives are formed from verbs by the addition of these suffixes:

> This is <u>boring</u>.   I feel <u>bored</u>.
> You are <u>annoying</u>.   I feel <u>annoyed</u>.
> There was a <u>roaring</u> scream as the twister completed its <u>plummeting</u> descent.

(See page 45 on adjectives.)

Nouns can also be formed from verbs by adding an '–ing' suffix:

> <u>Smoking</u> is prohibited.
> <u>Drinking</u> is on the increase.
> <u>Overeating</u> leads to obesity.

Substitution test

The substitution test shows whether a particular word – or letter string – functions as a verb, adjective or noun, if it can be replaced by a more familiar word from that class. For example,

> I feel annoyed/happy. (adjective)
> I annoyed/met my parents. (verb)
> Drinking/Crime is on the increase. (noun)
> She was drinking/making coffee. (verb)

A further substitution test for nouns is to see whether the word can be replaced by a pronoun:

> *Drinking/It is on the increase. (noun)*

Nonsense rhymes can be used to practise identifying the role of word classes. Activity 6.4 is a parody of Lewis Carroll's poem 'Jabberwocky'.

Activity 6.4

Many of the invented words in this poem are nouns – names from computer games.

- Identify the invented verbs.
- Note the use of verb suffixes, such as '–ed' or '–ing'. (form)
- Replace each with a more familiar verb. (function)

> ### Joystick Jabberwocky
>
> 'Twas Billy, and the Shyguy Clones
> Did Grax and Grumple in the Kraid;
> All Lizzie were the Hanger Zones,
> And Phanto Renegade.
>
> 'Beware the Shadow Boss, my son!
> The Killer Clams, the Mummy Men!
> Don't Goombah with a Neul, and shun
> The Death Breath known as Ken!'
>
> He Holtzed at Zigmos from afar,
> Dodged Zombie Slime with lightning scroll,
> While Zelda in her Mamda Jar
> Made Yuki with a Troll.
>
> And as he Beaked for Pyradoks,
> The Shadow Boss Twinbellowed through,
> Backed up by Pengs, Chicago Ox,
> Twelve Ninjas and McGoo.
>
> Dagoom! Dagoom! Zabs met their doom!
> And when the final Folfu fell,
> Lay Bloopered ranks of Battletanks
> And Mario as well.
>
> (Frank Jacobs, www.76.pair.com/keithlim/jabberwocky/parodies/joystick.html)

The following summary applies to *main* verbs. Chapter 8 will provide further understanding of the role of verbs in phrases, introducing the concepts of *auxiliary* verb, perfect and continuous aspects, passive and active voice, and indicative, imperative, conditional and subjunctive mood.

TABLE 6.1 Main verbs summary

Function	can be replaced by other verbs
Form	take suffixes, such as '–s', '–ing', '–ed'
Meaning	express actions or states

The next section deals with the remaining content classes: adjectives and adverbs.

Adjectives and adverbs

Adjectives and adverbs can be explored together, as they are similar in some important ways. They are – nearly always – optional elements in the structure of sentences. Because of this, these two word classes are significant for style.

Key words

adjective: comparative, superlative

Language in use

I notice that you use plain, simple language, short words and brief sentences. That is the way to write English – it is the modern way and the best way. Stick to it; don't let fluff and flowers and verbosity creep in. When you catch an adjective, kill it. No, I don't mean utterly, but kill most of them – then the rest will be valuable. They weaken when they are close together. They give strength when they are wide apart. An adjective habit, or a wordy, diffuse, flowery habit, once fastened upon a person, is as hard to get rid of as any other vice. (Mark Twain, Letter 1880)

If it is possible to cut a word out, always cut it out. (George Orwell, Politics and the English Language)

As pupils develop their repertoire, the use of **adjectives** and adverbs can create more elaborate ways of expressing themselves in writing. However, experienced writers, such as Mark Twain and George Orwell above, often advise restraint in the use of such optional extras. When redrafting descriptive writing, pupils could check for overuse of adjectives, in particular. Some may be redundant; the use of well-chosen verbs or nouns can also convey vivid description. First, pupils need ways of identifying adjectives and adverbs. This section will follow a similar approach, exploring the usefulness of definitions based on meaning, form and function.

What is an adjective?

The familiar *meaning* definition of an adjective is 'a describing word'. This is not reliable, as the example in the introduction shows:

> *The drunk tottered into the alley clutching a whisky bottle under his raincoat.*

There are no adjectives in this sentence, but description is provided by nouns such as 'drunk' and 'alley' and the verbs 'tottered' and 'clutching'.

It is more useful to concentrate on the *function* of adjectives in relation to other words in the structure. Adjectives provide more detail about nouns. In English structure, adjectives generally operate in two positions: either before nouns, or after verbs expressing states – 'to be', 'to seem', etc.

Another feature of adjectives is that more than one can be used in a list. The number is infinite in theory, but limited by considerations of style.

Insertion test

The insertion test can be used to collect a store of familiar adjectives in these two positions in English structure.

Activity 6.5

- What words can be added to these sentences?
- Can you add more than one word?

  This is a _____ coat.
  This coat seems _____ .

Substitution test

Pupils can use their store of known adjectives in substitution tests to check the role of apparently 'descriptive' words.

Activity 6.6

- Are the underlined words adjectives?
- Replace them with known adjectives – the structure should remain grammatical.

  The <u>drunk</u> tottered into the alley, <u>clutching</u> a whisky bottle under his raincoat.
  I saw a <u>drunk</u> figure and a <u>clutching</u> hand at the entrance of the subway.

Deletion test

The deletion test is the most useful way of identifying adjectives. As adjectives are optional elements, they can often be removed without destroying the structure.

NB Remember that *adverbs* are also optional extras. Further tests are needed to distinguish these two word classes.

Activity 6.7

- Underline the words that can be removed from this horoscope.
- Use the substitution test to check whether they are adjectives.

> **Leo**
>
> *Spiritual retreat or dancing feet? Two contrasting themes are emphasised in your current horoscope. While planets in the adjacent sign of Cancer demand you spend time communing with your inner Lion, the presence of Venus in Leo calls for you to sport the gaudiest items in your wardrobe and hit the town. There's a rewarding intensity to either pursuit this week, but since you'll be partying hard in a month's time, make sure the priory is a priority now.*

Form

Pupils' knowledge of morphology can be used to identify adjectives. Certain suffixes indicate a change from a noun or verb to an adjective:

	noun	*adjective*
–ious	caution	caut*ious*
–ful	beauty	beauti*ful*
–ent	intelligence	intellig*ent*
–al	person	person*al*
–y	wind	wind*y*

	verb	*adjective*
–ing	annoy	annoy*ing*
–ed	bore	bor*ed*

Adjectives themselves can change form in two ways to show **comparative** and **superlative**.

The suffix '–er' is added to some adjectives to compare their quality with another:

> *This car is bigger than the one I usually drive.*

The suffix '–est' is added if more than two things are being compared:

> *This is the biggest car I have ever driven.*

This knowledge of the form of adjectives can be used in an insertion test. An unfamiliar word, such as 'slithy' or 'mimsy' from 'The Jabberwocky' (Lewis Carroll), can take the comparative and superlative form: 'slithier' or 'mimsiest'.

Applications to standard English

There are, of course, exceptions to these two rules that cause some non-standard forms of adjectives. For example,

gooder, bestest, beautifullest, most favouritest, more harder, deader

Pupils should be aware of the exceptions to the rule. Two common adjectives are irregular:

good, better, best
bad, worse, worst

Adjectives with more than two syllables generally use 'more' or 'most' in place of a suffix:

more beautiful, most favourite

Adjectives do not take *both* a suffix *and* a modifier:

more lovely   or   lovelier

Some adjectives cannot be compared; they're absolute:

dead, pregnant, perfect

Application to style

As adjectives are optional extras in English structure, it is a matter of stylistic choice. In descriptive writing, pupils learn to use adjectives to add effective detail. However, they should be aware that a plain style may also be effective. Writers may also convey a vivid scene by the use of effective nouns and verbs.

Activity 6.8

Which adjectives could be deleted before the nouns (underlined)?

> <u>Time</u> stood still as the rosy red <u>ribbon</u> of early morning <u>sunlight</u> stretched lazily over the dusty <u>scrubland</u> below us. A blurry <u>haze</u> was already rising above the scorched yellow <u>stubble</u>, threatening an oppressive and overbearing <u>heat</u>. <u>Families</u> of elegant <u>impala</u>, <u>kudu</u> and <u>eland</u> were grazing peacefully on the sparse <u>vegetation</u> below, their <u>predators</u> already having taken refuge in the little <u>shelter</u> they could find. Lolling idly in the withered <u>turf</u>, their dusty golden <u>bodies</u> were cleverly camouflaged.
>
> *(student work)*

TABLE 6.2 Adjectives summary

Function	can be inserted before nouns, or after stative verbs
	more than one can be inserted in these positions
	can often be deleted
Form	can take a comparative or superlative form
	certain suffixes indicate a change in word class to adjectives
Meaning	add detail to the noun

What are adverbs?

Adverbs are the most varied and flexible of the word classes, performing a range of functions. The familiar definition of an adverb refers to both its meaning and its function: 'an adverb describes a verb and tells you how, when or where it happened'. It is true that adverbs often function with verbs, but they have another important role in English structure – adverbs also function to qualify adjectives or other adverbs. Pupils should become aware that, as optional extras, adverbs have an effect on style.

Key words
adverb   connective   intensifier

Language in use

What would make 2005 a good year for you and your school?
I'm not looking forward to 2005 too much because I've got my GCSEs. My big hope is that they go well. I'm a bit dodgy on subjects like French: too many genders, too many accents. But my Maths and sciences aren't bad and I'd really like good grades for those. It would be nice if our football team could win a bit more often. We aren't bad, but we could do with more practice. That might make a difference. If we could have a new sports stadium with a pool and a gym, that would be pretty good too, but it won't happen because there's no space and I shouldn't think there's any money, either.

(Jamie Bird, 15, writing in the Guardian*)*

The overuse of **adverbs**, particularly the colloquial 'just' and 'really', is a common feature of pupils' writing. The above example uses many adverbs, which are effective in conveying the personal feelings of the writer in a spontaneous, informal way. In more formal situations, however, the writer might remove the impressionistic adverbs: 'too much', 'bit', 'really', 'pretty'. In order to make these choices, pupils should be able to identify adverbs.

What is an adverb?

Adverbs are closely related to adjectives in *form*, as many adverbs are formed by adding the suffix '–ly' to an adjective:

> *warmly, independently, graciously, thankfully, really*

In these cases, it is straightforward to identify adverbs by their form. However, many adverbs do not have this recognisable form:

> *now, just, hard, very, always, too, so*

One *function* of adverbs is to provide more information about the verb – where, when or how it happened.

Deletion and transposition tests

Like adjectives, adverbs are optional elements in the structure, so can be deleted. The unique feature of adverbs is their moveability. Adverbs can be moved to various positions in English structure:

- immediately before the verb
- after the verb
- between parts of the verb phrase
- at the beginning of the structure
- at the end of the structure.

These features of adverbs are shown in the following activity, which returns to the extract used to identify adjectives.

Activity 6.9

Identify the adverbs in the following passage. This time the verbs are underlined.

You have seen in Activity 6.8 (page 83) that adjectives occurring before nouns can be deleted.

- Which other words can be deleted from the structure?
- Which ones seem unnecessary?
- What position can adverbs take in the structure?

> Time <u>stood</u> still as the rosy red ribbon of early morning sunlight <u>stretched</u> lazily over the dusty scrubland below us. A blurry haze <u>was</u> already <u>rising</u> above the scorched yellow stubble, <u>threatening</u> an oppressive and overbearing heat. Families of elegant impala, kudu and eland <u>were grazing</u> peacefully on the sparse vegetation below, their predators already <u>having taken refuge</u> in the little shelter they <u>could find</u>. <u>Lolling</u> idly in the withered turf, their dusty golden bodies <u>were</u> cleverly <u>camouflaged</u>.

Transposition

Many adverbs do not have the easily recognisable form – the suffix '–ly'. The transposition test is a reliable way of checking whether a word functions as an adverb. The meaning definition can be used to support this conclusion.

Activity 6.10

Identify the adverbs in the sentences below.

- Which words can be moved to other positions in the structure? (function)
- What sort of detail do they convey? (meaning)
- Does the form of the words provide a clue? (form)

Make sure you always bring a pen and paper.

Nowadays young people tend to rent, rather than buy, property.

I need to finish the essay tonight.

Applications to style

The previous activities showed the way adverbs can function to add detail about the time, place or manner of the action described by the verb. However, another important function of adverbs is as **connectives**, providing links between sentences. One example is the word 'however', used in the previous sentence. Other adverbs – and adverbial phrases – are commonly used to maintain the cohesion of a text. Like conjunctions, these adverbs express various relationships between sentences. (See Chapter 13 on discourse.)

TABLE 6.3 Adverbs summary

Addition	also, furthermore, moreover
Opposition	however, nevertheless, instead, on the other hand
Reinforcing	besides, anyway, after all
Explaining	for example, in other words, that is to say
Listing	first(ly), next, finally
Indicating result	therefore, consequently, as a result
Indicating time	just then, meanwhile, later

Another function of adverbs is to indicate the point of view of the writer or speaker.

We will <u>*hopefully*</u> *get tickets for Glastonbury.*

Some people object to this use of adverbs, as they do not qualify the verb – it is not the getting of tickets that is hopeful, but the feelings of the speaker. It is clearer to use these adverbs at the beginning or end of the structure:

<u>*Allegedly,*</u> *the accused bought the Rolex from a market stall.*

Although considered non-standard by some, this use of adverbs is common, even in more formal writing. This makes adverbs highly significant in implying meanings. The ability to identify adverbs can help pupils distinguish impersonal statements from expression of personal attitudes. The following extracts are taken from an article about the contemporary use of 'innit'.

Activity 6.11

■ Identify the adverbs used in the following sentences – the verbs are underlined.

■ Do they describe the verb, or the attitude of the writer?

– *There <u>is</u> some debate about the origins of the word 'innit'. The* Oxford English Dictionary *sniffily <u>records</u> it merely as a 'vulgar' version of 'isn't it'.*

– *There <u>is</u> an information bank for the study of teenage London English, the Corpus of London. Teenage Language (COLT), <u>based</u>, somewhat bizarrely, at the University of Bergen, Norway.*

– *Assiduous linguists <u>have</u> <u>recorded</u> and, more painfully, <u>transcribed</u> 'half-a-million words of spontaneous conversations'.*

Insertion test

Although adverbs of time and place can provide precise details, adverbs of manner often express personal opinions. For this reason, they are often omitted from texts with a formal, objective or authoritative tone, such as religious, academic, scientific or legal language. The effect on style can be shown, using the insertion test with colloquial adverbs.

Activity 6.12

■ Insert adverbs such as 'really', 'just', 'only', 'actually', 'honestly' into the following sentences.

■ What is the effect on the tone?

– *And God said, 'Let there be light.'*

– *Vertebrates are animals with a backbone.*

– *I promise to tell the truth, the whole truth and nothing but the truth.*

Adverbs used with adjectives

Although the term 'adverb' suggests its role with verbs, adverbs are also commonly used to modify adjectives. The term **intensifier** is often used for this function of adverbs. This is because they usually express the degree – or intensity – of the adjective:

> *The handwriting was*   *barely*   *legible.*
> *fairly*
> *quite*
> *reasonably*
> *perfectly*

Adverbs can also occur before other adverbs, performing a similar function:

> *Please write*   *very*   *legibly.*

In the examples above, intensifiers were used to differentiate degrees of legibility. Often, however, intensifiers do not convey anything precise or objective. They express a vague sense of emphasis, so are more common in colloquial speech than in writing. The choice of a particular intensifier tends to reflect the social identity of the writer or speaker.

Activity 6.13

- Which of the following intensifiers would you use?
- Which ones would you never use?
- What does each suggest about the identity of the speaker?

> *That was*   *very*   *good.*
> *so*
> *jolly*
> *really*
> *incredibly*
> *right*
> *dead*
> *well*
> ******
>
> *(plus some taboo words!)*

TABLE 6.4 Adverbs summary

Function	can occur with verbs – can be deleted or transposed
	can occur before adjectives or other adverbs – can be deleted
Form	may be formed by adding the suffix '–ly' to adjectives
Meaning	express meanings such as time, place and manner with verbs
	express degrees of intensity with adjectives

7

Noun phrases

The next two chapters move up to the third level of structure – the way words combine to form phrases.

TABLE 7.1 Levels of structure

One or more **morphemes**	combine to form	words.
One or more **words**	combine to form	phrases.
One or more **phrases**	combine to form	clauses.
One or more **clauses**	combine to form	sentences.
One or more **sentences**	combine to form	paragraphs and whole texts.

In some ways, the best starting point for grammar study is with phrases, as this is where the structure of language becomes obvious. A sentence may look like a chain of individual words on the surface, but is, in fact, a more complex three-dimensional structure. As the examples in the Introduction showed, phrases (and clauses) are often embedded beneath the surface. These two sentences have the same underlying structure of four phrases.

> [Teenagers] [upset] [me] [now].
> [The rowdy behaviour of teenagers] [has been upsetting] [the whole family] [for the past year].

The term 'phrase' suggests a group of words, but it is more helpful to think of a phrase as a unit. Like a family, a phrase may consist of a single member – word – but can expand to include related elements within the unit. So the single noun teenagers is expanded into a longer phrase; 'the rowdy behaviour of teenagers'.

Just as market research uses the concept of the 'head' of the household, phrases are classified according to the headword. There are five types of phrases, each associated with the content word classes: noun, verb, adjective and adverb, as well as prepositional phrases.

TABLE 7.2

Noun phrases	the rowdy *behaviour* of teenagers
	the whole *family*
Verb phrase	has been *upsetting*
Prepositional phrase	*for* the past year

Study of phrase structure helps to consolidate pupils' understanding of the role of word classes – nouns are usually grouped with determiners and adjectives; and main verbs often occur with auxiliary verbs.

Phrases are a significant feature of language variation. Awareness of simple and complex phrases can be applied to reading skills. Pupils should notice how some writers of fiction use a plain style, whereas others employ more detailed description. The use of complex noun phrases is a feature of formal, academic styles – more so than the use of complex sentence structures. This awareness can be applied to pupils' own writing, as they are rewarded in SATs mark schemes for the use of more complex phrases.

> **Year 7:** expand nouns and noun phrases, e.g. by using a prepositional phrase

> **Year 9:** know and use the terms that are useful for analysing language, e.g. type of phrase, conditional verb

Pupils also need to develop their ability to use a range of verb phrases to express various aspects of time in narratives. Writing to persuade often involves expression of hypothetical or suggested ideas. In English grammar, aspects of time, conditional and subjunctive meanings are expressed by the expansion of the verb phrase (rather than the many different verb endings used in Romance languages).

This chapter deals with noun, preposition, adjective and adverb phrases. Chapter 8 explores verb phrases.

Noun phrase structure

> **Year 9:** know and use the terms that are useful for analysing language e.g. type of phrase

This section explores the structure of noun phrases, beginning with the basic element of a single noun and showing the ways this can be expanded by the insertion of other elements. These may be single words – determiners and adjectives – as Chapter 6 showed. But more complex noun phrases are formed by adding other phrases, or even clauses.

Key words
noun phrase   headword   modifier   postmodification   prepositional phrase

---

Language in use

ANGST-RIDDEN MELODIC SCREAMY METAL-CORE

(flyer advertising a music gig)

Hydroterapia detoxifying moisturised sea salts

(product name/label on bottle)

Bargain sofa hunters. If you missed the DFS December Sale, Double Discount Boxing Day Sale, January Clearance Sale and the February End of Winter Sale, don't worry – the Spring Sale starts in March.

(parody of sales promotions in Viz)

The most simple **noun phrase** is a single noun. In the examples above, the key nouns are:

metal-core, salts, sale

The term **headword** is used in many grammar books to refer to the essential role of this key element of each phrase.

As the examples above of promotional language show, the noun phrase can be expanded to provide more precise, enticing details. The bottle, for example, does not simply contain 'salts', but a particular – even unique – product:

sea <u>salts</u>
moisturised sea <u>salts</u>
detoxifying moisturised sea <u>salts</u>
Hydroterapia detoxifying moisturised sea <u>salts</u>

All three examples use this structure of noun phrases: the insertion of words *before* the noun.

> **Year 7:** expand nouns and noun phrases

Insertion test

An activity such as the following uses the insertion test to show the type of words that can be used to expand noun phrases in this way.

Activity 7.1

- Name some objects you can see in the room.
- Begin with the single noun and add more detail before the noun.

> *Example*
>
> *Cup*
>
> This cup.

> *This plastic cup.*
> *This white plastic cup.*
> *This crumpled white plastic cup.*
> *This crumpled white plastic coffee cup.*

- What types of words can come before the noun to make a longer phrase?

Noun phrases as titles

Noun phrases usually occur as part of full sentence structures, but it is helpful to look first at examples of noun phrases in isolation. Brand names provide a source of useful, contemporary examples: titles of films, books and TV programmes; names of products, bands, clubs, restaurants, etc. These are generally quite 'snappy', but people can go to absurd lengths to create impressive job titles. This example from Essex County Council was held up to ridicule in the media:

Decriminalisation of Parking Enforcement Project Implementation Manager
(Daily Mail, *16 February 2005*)

In the classroom, book titles can be used to consolidate pupils' awareness of noun phrase structure. Many follow the basic structure illustrated above: the headword alone, or one preceded by determiners and / or **modifiers**:

> *Holes*
> The *Odyssey*
> Good *Bones*
> The Wrong *Boy*
> The No. 1 Ladies Detective *Agency*

Activities such as the following demonstrate this common structure of noun phrases.

Activity 7.2

- Group the following titles of horror stories according to the noun phrase structure.
- Underline the headword and note the types of word used to expand the phrase.
- Use the terms 'determiner' and 'modifier'.

  - *The Shining*
  - *Prime Evil*
  - *Alien*
  - *The Animal Hour*

- *The Wyrm*
- *Midnight's Lair*
- *The Rats*
- *Endless Night*
- *Nightfall*
- *The Fog*
- *The Twilight Zone*

Teachers can consolidate pupils' awareness of this structure of noun phrases by creative activities such as the following.

Activity 7.3

Work in pairs for this activity. You are going to create some book titles and challenge another pair to identify the genre and provide a brief synopsis.

■ Select one word from each of the three groups to create some noun phrases.

■ Decide which genre of book each title will suit.

For example, if you have created *The Icy Hand*, it will probably be a horror book, but *The Icy Heart* would probably be a romance.

determiner	modifier	headword
the	green	hand
a	hot	foot
an	icy	shroud
my	glittering	heart
her	strange	stranger
our	dark	intruder
his	dead	knife
this	laughing	folly
some	lost	stone
that	stone	eye
your	burning	light
its	crimson	sky
	wild	mist
	heavy	train
	dripping	spell

Applications to style

Pupils are assessed for their ability to use more complex noun phrases. This is often done in descriptive writing by the addition of one or more adjectives before the headword. For example,

> black <u>clothes</u>
> the cold, frosty <u>air</u>
> Avril, a stupid immature <u>girl</u>
> an evil-looking and rather scary <u>poodle</u>

They should be aware, however, that a plain style may also be effective. The following activity shows the stylistic effects of two different styles of narrative.

Activity 7.4

- Identify the noun phrases used by each of the following writers.
- What do you notice about the differences in style?
- How much description is provided about the characters and the setting?

Extract 1

Nick stood up. He was all right. He looked up the track at the lights of the caboose going out of sight around the curve. There was water on both sides of the track, then tamarack swamp. He felt his knee. The pants were torn and the skin was barked. His hands were scraped and there were sand and cinders driven up under the nails. He went over to the edge of the track down the little slope to the water and washed his hands. He washed them carefully in the cold water, getting the dirt out from the nails. He squatted down and bathed his knee.

(Hemingway, The Battler)

Extract 2

The three brothers and the sister sat round the desolate breakfast-table, attempting some sort of desultory consultation. The morning's post had given the final tap to the family fortunes, and all was over. The dreary dining-room itself, with its heavy mahogany furniture, looked as if it were waiting to be done away with. But the consultation amounted to nothing. There was a strange air of ineffectuality about the three men, as they sprawled at table, smoking and reflecting vaguely on their own condition. The girl was alone, a rather short, sullen-looking young woman of twenty-seven. She did not share the same life as her brothers.

(D.H Lawrence, The Horse Dealer's Daughter)

Expanding noun phrases after the headword

So far, we have looked at noun phrases which have all the extra detail inserted before the key noun. The other way to expand noun phrases is by adding detail after the noun. Some grammar books use the term **postmodification** for this structure. In the structure of some languages, it is common to place adjectives after the noun, but this is very rare in English grammar. The few examples are often influenced by French:

> *heir apparent*
> *Little Boy Blue*

Year 7: expand nouns and noun phrases, e.g. by using a prepositional phrase

The following examples were used in the Ryanair magazine, but the writer is not a native speaker of English:

> *It is a journey strange and a journey bold. But be assured it will be a journey magical.*

The use of this unusual structure tends to draw attention to itself – it is stylistically marked. The opening sentence of *Pride and Prejudice* (Jane Austen) provides a well-known example:

> *It is a truth universally acknowledged, that a single man in possession of a large fortune, must be in want of a wife.*

The usual structure would be:

> *It is a universally acknowledged truth . . .*

If an adjective is placed after the noun, it is usually part of a phrase:

> *the cup, full of water, . . .*

The use of phrases to add detail after the noun is very common in English structure. Examples from the previous extracts (see page 94) follow a similar pattern:

> *the lights of the caboose*
> *both sides of the track*
> *the edge of the track*
> *a strange air of ineffectuality*

The type of phrases used in this role are called **prepositional phrases**, because a preposition – 'of' – is used to link the key noun with another noun phrase.

Insertion test

The following activity demonstrates this common way of expanding noun phrases: by inserting a phrase after the key noun.

Year 7: expand nouns and noun phrases, e.g. by using a prepositional phrase

Activity 7.5

- Choose a noun phrase from the following list of examples.
- Add another noun phrase, using a preposition to connect the two.

(Example

noun phrase	+	*preposition*	+	*noun phrase*
the thing		with		some peculiar habits)

noun phrases

my old dog	knobbly knees
batter	strange green bits
the last train	green slime
some peculiar habits	this mars bar
the thing	the vicar
chocolate sauce	hairy nostrils
a very desirable residence	calories
purple silk cycling shorts	an extra leg
cold fried eggs	the extremely fat man
a six-lane motorway	that tower block

Prepositions

in, on, of, with, by, under, over, through

Application to style

Although it often assumed that complex sentence structures are a feature of formal writing, recent research based on a large corpus of texts showed a different type of complexity. Formal writing often uses complex noun phrases within a basic sentence structure. The following examples are taken from an academic text on language, and an article written by a 15-year-old boy, who won a place at Cambridge University. The sentence structures are, in fact, quite simple. It is the expanded noun phrases that increase the level of complexity.

Activity 7.6

- How are the key nouns (underlined) expanded into more precise phrases?

> **Extract 1**
>
> Language is moderately good at conveying simple _pieces_ of factual information. Such information _talking_ is assumed to be at the _core_ of language. Yet its _efficiency_ in this role depends on the _type_ of information being conveyed.
>
> (Jean Aitchison, The Seeds of Speech)

> **Extract 2**
>
> There are aspects that can be seen as early _manifestations_ of my dyslexic problems and my _escape_ into literature. I remember a _feeling_ which permeated everything. It was a _sense_, right from the _beginning_, when I started to socialise with other children, that I was in some way different.
>
> (Alexander Faludy, Guardian)

Using clauses to expand noun phrases

The previous activity showed a further way of expanding noun phrases – by inserting _clauses_ after the key noun.

> _Its efficiency in this role depends on the type of information being conveyed._
> _I remember a feeling which permeated everything._

Tests

How can we tell that the clause is part of the noun phrase? The tests of deletion, substitution and insertion can be used.

Deletion test: What parts of the structure can be removed, leaving the basic structure intact?

> _Its efficiency in this role depends on the type of information [being conveyed]._
> _I remember a feeling [which permeated everything]._

Substitution test: What does the pronoun 'it' replace?

> _Its efficiency depends on it [the type of information being conveyed]._
> _I remember it [a feeling which permeated everything]._

Although the use of subordinate clauses to expand a noun is a complex structure, it is commonly used and easily understood. Nursery rhymes and children's stories often use this structure:

> _This is the house [that Jack built]._
> _This is the rat [that lived in the house that Jack built]._
> _This is the cat [that killed the rat that lived in the house that Jack built]._

Insertion test: What words, phrases and clauses can be added to provide more precise detail to the key noun? The following activity might be used in the classroom.

Activity 7.7

- Compile a simple list of gifts you want for your birthday. These are single nouns. For example,

  trainers, PlayStation, CD, bike

- Now 'tell me what you really, really want' by adding precise detail. For example,

  What I really, really want is the latest PlayStation with a dual-control joypad, equipped with mega memory and replay facility.

- What have you inserted to expand the noun phrase?

Linking clauses to noun phrases

Clauses are linked to the noun phrase by connectives. The conjunctions often used in this role are 'which', 'who', 'that'.

> *This is the cat <u>which</u> chased the rat.*
> *This is the dog <u>who</u> killed the cat.*
> *This is the house <u>that</u> Jack built.*

NB In English grammar, it is possible to omit the conjunction 'that'.

> *This is the house [ ] Jack built.*

The other way of connecting clauses to the noun is the use of a verb with the suffix '–ing' or '–ed'.

> *a Playstation <u>equipped</u> with dual control*
> *the information <u>being</u> conveyed*

These verb forms are termed 'non-finite' – the present and past 'participle'. (See Chapter 9 on subordinate clauses.)

Applications to style

Some genres of writing use highly complex noun phrases for various reasons. Academic, technical or legal texts need to specify details to be as accurate and precise as possible. Advertisements, as seen at the beginning of this section (page 91), tend to include details to promote the product as desirable. The final activity in this section examines the use of noun phrases in the genre of estate agents' leaflets and suggests a writing activity for pupils.

Activity 7.8

The noun phrases have been marked by brackets, with the headword underlined.

- Why are the noun phrases in this estate agents' description complex?

Extract 1

[An immaculate spacious three-bedroom cottage-style terraced <u>property</u> with full gas-fired central heating] is on [the <u>market</u>] through [this estate <u>agency</u>]. [The ground floor <u>accommodation</u>] briefly comprises [a charming bay-windowed <u>lounge</u>, containing a superb late Victorian slate feature fireplace with a living flame gas fire;] [a separate <u>dining-room</u> with fitted radiation gas fire;] [a well-fitted offshot <u>kitchen</u> containing high-quality fitted hygena units, Worcester Heatslave gas-fired combination boiler and plumbing for an automatic washer].

- Your task is to write an estate agents' description of the following property, to entice someone to buy it. Use extended noun phrases as in the example above.

Extract 2

Nightmare Hall has recently come on to the market. It looks like the sort of old haunted house that sensible people keep away from in horror films. On one side runs the M500, a ten-lane motorway. On the other side is the local sewage works. Nightmare Hall has about 25 bedrooms – the owner, Count Blood, can't remember the exact number, and he's difficult to contact as he refuses to make appointments during the day – extensive kitchens, a ballroom and a banqueting hall on the ground floor. It is well supplied with cellars and crypts, the crypts containing the tombs of members of the Blood family. It has no heating apart from a huge fire in the banqueting hall, very little plumbing, and has probably never been decorated.

TABLE 7.3 Noun phrases summary

Substitution	A noun phrase can be replaced by a preposition.
Insertion	A single noun can be expanded in various ways: – determiner and modifiers before the key noun – prepositional phrases after the key noun – clauses after the key noun.
Deletion	Modifiers and postmodifiers can be removed from the structure. Determiners are usually essential and cannot be deleted.

The next section looks at the ways single adjectives and adverbs can be expanded into longer phrases.

Adjectival and adverbial phrases

Adjectival and adverbial phrases are relatively simple in structure. As pupils intuitively use and understand these phrases, it may not be necessary to provide explicit teaching of the forms. Their function may also seem obvious – to provide more detailed description. However, as optional elements, the use of adjectival and adverbial phrases has an effect on style. Pupils should be aware that the use of intensifiers creates a more personal, informal style.

Key words

adjectival phrase   adverbial phrase   intensifier

Language in use

But these <u>minor</u> worries could <u>hardly</u> compare with the consternation caused on the Monopoly front by a <u>swift-fingered</u> checker-out from a Bedford supermarket whose palm was <u>so</u> <u>extraordinarily</u> <u>speedy</u> in the recovery of the two dice thrown from the <u>cylindrical</u> cup that her opponents had <u>little</u> option to accept, without ever seeing the <u>slightest</u> evidence, her <u>instantaneously enunciated</u> score, and then to watch <u>helplessly</u> as this <u>sharp-faced</u> woman moved her <u>little</u> counter along the board to whichever square seemed of the <u>greatest potential</u> profit to her <u>entrepreneurial</u> designs.
(Colin Dexter, The Secret of Annexe 3, a Morse Mystery)

The example above uses adjectives and adverbs (underlined) to add descriptive detail to a scene in a novel. Unlike nouns or verbs, they usually occur as a single word:

He watched <u>helplessly</u>.

Form of phrases

There are only a few ways of expanding an adjective or adverb into a longer phrase. This is usually done by inserting words before the headword – premodification:

Her palm was [so extraordinarily] <u>speedy</u>.

There are only a few possibilities for postmodification:

Her palm was [very] <u>speedy</u> [indeed].

An activity such as the following can demonstrate the type of words that can be used in **adjectival** and **adverbial phrases**.

Activity 7.9

- Complete the sentences below by inserting as many different modifiers before the headword.
- What word class do these words belong to?
- Can you add any words after the headword to modify it further?

> *My cat is _____ lovely. (adjective)*
> *It sleeps _____ soundly. (adverb)*

Applications to style

The previous activity showed that adjectival and adverbial phrases can be expanded by adding adverbs. In this role, adverbs are sometimes called '**intensifiers**', as they indicate how lovely the cat is, or how soundly it sleeps. This is often a matter of style, rather than them adding precise information – it would be difficult to say which of the modifiers expressed the highest degree:

> *very/extremely/really/lovely*

As Chapter 6, page 88 showed, the use of intensifiers often reflects the speaker's, or writer's, background, as well as their attitude. For this reason, formal texts tend to avoid the use of these modifiers. Experienced writers may use them deliberately to convey an extreme, personal opinion in an informal style.

Activity 7.10

- Note the use of adverbs as intensifiers in the following extract from an article.
- What other features contribute to the informal style?
- What formal language features does the writer use in contrast?

> *Why does the BBC bother spending £5 million on* Fame Academy, *a new talent-based reality show for the autumn, when genetic experts can tell them it won't be as good as* Pop Idol *and that the public will see through another unimaginative attempt to rehash other people's more successful ideas, but in a slightly cack-handed BBC-ish way in which the corporation balks at being too brash, thus removing from the series those more tabloidish, voyeuristic elements that made* Pop Idol *so successful in the first place, the yellow-bellied, faux-populist dunderheads?*
>
> (Armando Iannucci, Guardian)

TABLE 7.4 Adjectival and adverbial phrases summary

Form	Adverbs can come before the headword.
	A few adverbs can come after the headword.
Function	These optional elements can be deleted.
	The phrase can often be replaced by a single word.
Meaning	The modifiers often 'intensify' the headword.

Chapter 8 explores the remaining type of phrase, discussing the ways a single main verb can be expanded into longer verb phrases to convey a range of meanings.

Verb phrases

This chapter explores verb phrases. Because the structure is governed by a few fixed rules, the terminology is more detailed. The shades of meaning conveyed by verb phrases are explained, using the concepts of *tense, aspect, mood* and *voice*.

Native language users operate this complex system of verbs intuitively, so teachers need to weigh the benefits of explicit knowledge against the drawbacks of 'too much information'. Even students of EFL or EAL (English as a Foreign Language or English as an Alternative Language) can acquire a functional use of English without knowing the terms for the structures. Teaching of foreign languages in schools today has also moved away from a structural approach – to the regret of some teachers!

For the sake of 'completeness', I have chosen to cover all the terms and concepts used in the National Literacy Strategy, but I am aware that this knowledge was gained over a lifetime. I hope that discerning readers will also make choices – to skip some sections, pick those that seem most useful for their pupils, and use the book for reference as necessary.

Structure of verb phrases

Key words
main verb   auxiliary verb

Language in use
The kidnappers stalked a local man. *Two men were stalking the girl in the park.* *She had been stalking him for two days.* *Nadia has been being stalked for the last day or so.* *You might have been being stalked by agents who just want to offer you membership.*

Verb phrase structure is relatively straightforward. The examples above show how a simple verb phrase – 'stalked' – can be expanded by the addition of modifiers. Compared to the flexibility of noun phrases, verb phrase structure is restricted to a few set patterns:

- Only verbs can be used as modifiers.
- Modifiers always come before the headword.
- The number of modifiers is limited to four.
- The order of modifiers is fixed.

Main vs auxiliary verbs

The patterns above move from the most simple to the most complex structure of verb phrases. The first important distinction is between main and auxiliary verbs. The term **main verb** is used for the key word that conveys the meaning, or content. The term **auxiliary verb** is used for the 'helping', or grammatical, words in the structure.

Auxiliary verbs				*Main verb*
				stalked
			were	*stalking*
		had	*been*	*stalking*
	has	*been*	*being*	*stalked*
might	*have*	*been*	*being*	*stalked*

Most verb functions can be expressed using no more than two auxiliary verbs. The first three combinations are those most frequently used to express present or past events. The final two structures involve the passive voice, with a conditional slant expressed in the most complex verb phrase. The use of four auxiliary verbs is possible in English grammar, but extremely rare in authentic language use.

Insertion test

Pupils' intuitive grasp of the common verb phrase structures can be demonstrated in activities such as the following. They can be asked to expand any single verb by inserting auxiliary verbs before the main verb.

Activity 8.1

At Ricotta's Great Flea Circus, you can see Fleas Jump!
- Use auxiliary verbs, such as 'be', 'have', 'will', 'might', etc.
- Create verb phrases by adding these to the main verb 'jump'.
  You may have to change the form of the main verb.
- What meanings do the different forms convey?

> **Example**
>
> *The fleas didn't jump. (past event)*
>
> *They might jump today. (possibility)*
>
> *The fleas are all jumping now. (ongoing action)*
>
> *That flea has just jumped. (recent event)*

Tense

The first way of classifying verbs is by **tense**. Unfortunately, this term is not used consistently. A common assumption is that tense is equivalent to *time*, with the distinction between past, present and future. In that case, there would be three tenses in language. If we turn to grammar texts for an explanation, there are conflicting opinions about the number of tenses in English: some say there are five, others seven, or even fourteen.

In this book, I use the technical definition: the term 'tense' refers to the distinction between *forms* of the main verb. Some languages, such as French, use different forms of the verb for many different tenses: present, future, past, imperfect, pluperfect, conditional, subjunctive. The English language only changes the form of the main verb to indicate a distinction between *present* and *past tense*. So there are two tenses in English.

Past tense	*Present tense*
I came, I saw, I conquered. (past)	*I come, I see, I conquer. (present)*

NB Future time is expressed by using **auxiliary verbs**.

> *I will conquer.*
> *I am going to conquer.*

The following activity demonstrates the two verb tenses in English and explores the relationship between tense and time.

Activity 8.2

- What suffixes do the verbs (underlined) take in the following extracts? (form)
- What aspect of time do they convey? (function)
- What is the term for these verb tenses?

Extract 1

The School-Boy

I _love_ to rise in a summer morn
When the birds _sing_ on every tree;
The distant hunstman _winds_ his horn,
And the sky-lark _sings_ with me:
O, what sweet company!

But to go to school in a summer morn,
O! it _drives_ all joy away;
Under a cruel eye outworn
The little ones _spend_ the day
In sighing and dismay.

(William Blake)

Extract 2

Rincewind _peered_ into the dark recesses of the Luggage. There _were_, indeed, among the chaos of boxes and bags of gold, several bottles and packages in oiled paper. He _gave_ a cynical laugh, _mooched_ around the abandoned jetty until he _found_ a piece of wood about the right length, _wedged_ it as politely as possible in the gap between the lid and the box, and pulled out one of the flat packages.

(Terry Pratchett, The Colour of Magic)

Applications to style

Year 8: explore the effects of changes in tense, e.g. past to present for vividness

In a straightforward world, the term 'present tense' would mean that it refers to the present time. However, this is not strictly accurate. The present tense can be used to convey various meanings.

1   The most common function of the simple present tense is to refer to regular events.

> I _love_ to rise in a summer morn
> When the birds _sing_ on every tree;

2   The present tense can also be used to convey a sense of immediacy or timelessness. Oral and written narratives, for example, may use the present tense to recount past events, sometimes referred to as the 'dramatic' present.

So, I go up to the manager and demand my wages. She just gives me the same old excuses.

NB Omission of '–s' for third person is an indication of a dialectal variation, in this case Black English Vernacular (BEV).

One bright Sunday morning in July I have trouble with my Notting Hill landlord because he ask for a month's rent in advance. (Jean Rhys, 'Let Them Call it Jazz')

3. Newspaper headlines may also use the present tense for past events.

Nelson Mandela speaks to the crowd in Trafalgar Square yesterday.

4. Scientific facts are presented as universal truths in the present tense.

Water freezes at 0 degrees.
Mammals breastfeed their young.

Application to standard English

Although pupils use most verb structures without problem, there is a significant variation between standard and non-standard English in the use of the auxiliary 'to do'. The use of a **'double negative'** is considered non-standard in English grammar and thus inappropriate in formal contexts.

Year 8: understand the main differences between standard English and dialectal variations, e.g. negatives

I didn't do nothing.

The explanation for this rule is often based on mathematics: two negatives make a positive. This rule, however, cannot be applied to language, as many languages use two negatives as the standard grammatical structure.

Je ne sais pas.

Although non-standard in English grammar, double negatives are used for emphasis, rather than to cancel each other out. It is important for pupils to recognise such structures as a non-standard, or dialectal, variation. They may occur in scripted dialogue to convey the speaker's social or educational background.

Activity 8.3

■ Identify the use of double negatives in the following extracts.

■ What does this suggest about the character?

> *My Gran never took Mark and Sonia to none of her special places after that. She only ever took me to those places.*

> *But it wasn't my fault neither; it wasn't my fault that I'd got all the blame for what had happened at the canal. It wasn't my fault that I didn't have no friends any more and that my best friend had betrayed me and dug up and ripped up the secret document.*
>
> *(Willy Russell, The Wrong Boy)*

Referring to the future

Other languages have a future tense – the form of the main verb changes by the addition of suffixes. Although there is no verb ending to indicate future time in English, there are various auxiliary verbs used to refer to the future.

Activity 8.4

- What auxiliary verbs are used to refer to future time in the following extracts?
- If you replace one auxiliary with another, does it affect the meaning?

> **Extract 1**
>
> *I have a dream that my four children will one day live in a nation where they will not be judged by the color of their skin but by the content of their character.*
>
> *(Martin Luther King, 'I Have a Dream')*

> **Extract 2**
>
> *These are my New Year's Resolutions:*
>
> *1   I will help the blind across the road.*
>
> *2   I will hang my trousers up.*
>
> *3   I will put the sleeves back on my records.*
>
> *(Sue Townsend, The Secret Diary of Adrian Mole aged 13³/₄)*

> **Extract 3**
>
> *When you become senile you won't know it.*
>
> *(Bill Cosby)*

> **Extract 4**
>
> *Blessed are the meek: for they shall inherit the earth.*
>
> *Blessed are they which do hunger and thirst after righteousness: for they shall be filled.*
>
> *(Matthew 5)*

Extract 5

When I am an old woman I shall wear purple

With a red hat which doesn't go, and doesn't suit me.

And I shall spend my pension on brandy and summer gloves.

(Jenny Joseph, 'Warning')

Extract 6

I am going to throw the trash out the closed window Stage.

I am going to help cook Stage.

I am going to rearrange the whole house Stage.

I am going to hide all your pretty little goodies Stage.

I am going to swipe all the goodies Stage.

I am going to kill everyone Stage.

(Alzheimers Support Websiter,
www.groups.msn.com/AlzheimersSupport/thepariensstages.msnw)

Applications to language variation and change

The most common auxiliary used for future time is 'going to'. This expresses the speaker's intentions:

> *I'm going to travel by train.*

Non-native speakers tend to choose the simpler form 'will'.

> *I will travel by train.*

But this auxiliary verb is used by native speakers to express more certainty, often unrelated to the speaker's intentions:

> *The train will arrive at platform five.*

It is also possible to use the present *simple* or present *continuous,* if the context makes the future reference clear.

Present simple to express future time:

> *Today was the most terrible day of my life. My mother has got a job doing her rotten typing in an insurance office! She <u>starts</u> on Monday! Mr Lucas works at the same place. He is going to give her a lift every day.*
>
> > *(Sue Townsend,* The Secret Diary of Adrian Mole aged 13³/₄*)*

Present continuous (see page 110) to express future time:

> *It's my mother's birthday on Saturday. <u>I'm organising</u> a surprise party.*

The conventions for using the auxiliary verbs 'will' as opposed to 'shall' have changed in recent years. At one time, it was standard English to use 'shall' for first person and 'will' for second and third person.

> I <u>shall</u> ask for a day off.
> You/He/She/They <u>will</u> ask for a day off.

The use of 'shall' for second or third person was, thus, stylistically marked as emphatic.

> Cinderella, you <u>shall</u> go to the ball.
> We <u>shall</u> overcome someday.

However, in contemporary language use, 'shall' is comparatively rare. It has been replaced by 'will' in most cases. Although a search engine, such as Google, produces thousands of examples of 'shall', many are taken from crafted written language, such as song lyrics, poems or speeches. It tends to convey a more stylised effect, or suggest an older style of language.

Verb aspects

Key words
aspect: continuous, perfect

This section will be brief, as explicit knowledge of verb **aspect** is not necessary for pupils at Key Stages 3 and 4. Native English speakers instinctively use all these forms appropriately. However, teachers make like to be familiar with the terminology. It is used in TESOL – Teaching English to Speakers of Other Languages – and may be used in A level language courses. These six aspects bring the number of verb phrase structures to eight:

	continuous	*perfect*	*perfect continuous*
present	*I am jumping*	*I have jumped*	*I have been jumping*
past	*I was jumping*	*I had jumped*	*I had been jumping*

These refer to various aspects of time: whether the action is ongoing or seen from a recent perspective.

> *Simple present/past*
> *Do you drink beer? (ever)*   *Are you drinking beer? (at this moment)*
> *I wrote my essay. (last night)*   *I was writing my essay. (all night)*
> *She was in hospital. (last week)*   *She has been in hospital. (sometime)*
> *My friend left the party. (at 11pm)*   *My friend had left the party. (before I arrived)*

Rather than using a complex system of suffixes, as happens in Romance languages such as French, Italian or Spanish, English grammar uses more complex verb phrases. These two auxiliary verbs are inserted before the headword:

> *to be*
> *to have*

Continuous

The verb 'to be' is used to convey **continuous** – or ongoing – actions either in the present or past. The main verb takes the suffix '–ing'.

> *I am listening to radio. I was waiting for hours.*

NB Some grammar books use the term 'progressive' rather than 'continuous'.

Perfect

The verb 'to have' is used to convey a recent perspective either in the present or past. The main verb takes the suffix '–ed' (or irregular forms of the past participle).

> *The train has left.*
> *I realised my watch had disappeared.*

The term for this aspect is **perfect**.

The two auxiliary verbs can be combined to form the present perfect continuous and the past perfect continuous. The main verb takes the suffix '–ing'.

> *I have been waiting for hours now.*
> *She had been hoping he would phone.*

Verb moods

Key words
mood: indicative, imperative, subjunctive, conditional modal auxiliary verb

The eight verb phrase structures in previous examples were all in the **indicative** mood: expressing events actually happening over various periods of time.

1	*Simple present*	*I listen to the radio.*
2	*Simple past*	*I waited for hours.*
3	*Present continuous*	*I am listening to radio.*
4	*Past continuous*	*I was waiting for hours.*

5	Present perfect	The train has left.
6	Past perfect	I realised my watch had disappeared.
7	Present perfect continuous	I have been waiting for hours now.
8	Past perfect continuous	She had been hoping he would phone.

There are three other **moods** for verbs in English.

The term **imperative** refers to verbs expressing commands, instructions and requests.

Leave me alone. Don't ask me again.

<table>
<tr><td>**Year 7:** revise the stylistic conventions of the main types of non-fiction; instructions which employ imperative verbs</td><td>The form of the imperative is very simple in English; it is the base form of the verb without any suffixes or auxiliary verbs. The negative is formed with 'don't'.</td></tr>
</table>

The term **subjunctive** refers to hypothetical situations, such as 'If I ruled the world...'

In languages such as French and Italian, there are separate subjunctive tenses with complex verb endings. In contemporary English, there is little evidence of verb forms that mark out a subjunctive mood, but some set phrases remain, using forms of the verb 'to be'.

subjunctive	indicative
if I were you	if I was you
as it were	as it is/was
so be it	so it is
be that as it may	that is as it is

Other verbs in English 'borrow' the past tense form to indicate that a situation is hypothetical, rather than a definite possibility:

hypothetical	definite possibility
if I ruled the world	if I rule the world

<table>
<tr><td>**Year 8:** recognise and exploit the use of conditionals and modal verbs when speculating, hypothesising or discussing possibilities</td><td>The term **conditional** is often used to label forms of verbs that indicate events that are possible under certain conditions.

When speculating, or hypothesising, pupils will intuitively change the form of the verb from its usual indicative by inserting other auxiliary verbs. They can demonstrate this in response to</td></tr>
</table>

questions introduced by 'if' or 'suppose'. The following activity makes this awareness explicit.

Activity 8. 5

■ Ask other people about these situations:

| If the school/college is closed on Monday... | (real possibility) |
| Suppose you won the lottery... | (possible in theory) |

■ What auxiliary verbs do they use?

Modal auxiliary verbs

Apart from the three primary auxiliary verbs mentioned earlier ('to be', 'to have', 'to do'), there is another group of auxiliary verbs. This group of **modal auxiliary verbs** have significant effects on meaning. They are used to convey various notions such as possibility, probability, necessity or obligation.

can	*could*
will	*would*
shall	*should*
may	*might*
must	*ought to*

Form and functions

These ten modal auxiliary verbs never change in form. No suffixes are added for the third person (* 'she cans'), or for changes to aspect (* 'I am maying'; * 'we have musted'). The grouping in pairs above shows that the second form can sometimes be used as the past tense.

There are a few other verbs that function as modal auxiliaries, expressing similar meanings. Their form, however, is slightly different. These verbs do change form, adding the suffixes '–s', '–ing' and '–ed'.

have to	*she has to/is having to/had to*
need to	*he needs to/was needing to/needed to*

Modal verbs express a variety of meanings, with subtle shades of meaning and some overlap. This makes their use in texts significant and worth close examination.

Possibility–probability

Some modal verbs indicate the degree of possibility of an event. Some of the verbs were listed in pairs above, with the second form sometimes used as the past tense. For example,

I can ride a bike.	*I could ride a bike when I was five years old.*
I will be famous one day.	*I always thought I would be famous.*
We shall be free.	*I believed we should be free.*
I may go to university.	*My parents hoped I might go to university.*

Apart from expressing either present or past time, these verbs express the attitude of the speaker to the degree of possibility of that event happening.

I will be famous.
I could be famous.
I may be famous.
I might be famous.

One use of the modal verb 'must' is to convey this type of conjecture.

> She _must_ have left.　　　　(*I suppose she has left.*)

When reading texts, pupils should be able to identify the use of modal verbs and explain the attitudes implied. This is particularly useful in analysis of persuasive texts.

Activity 8.6

- What modal verbs are used in this extract from a speech by Martin Luther King?
- What degree of possibility do they convey?

> We cannot walk alone. And as we walk, we must make the pledge that we shall march ahead. We cannot turn back. There are those who are asking the devotees of civil rights, 'When will you be satisfied?' We can never be satisfied as long as our bodies, heavy with the fatigue of travel, cannot gain lodging in the motels of the highways and the hotels of the cities. We cannot be satisfied as long as the Negro's basic mobility is from a smaller ghetto to a larger one. We can never be satisfied as long as a Negro in Mississippi cannot vote and a Negro in New York believes he has nothing for which to vote. No, no, we are not satisfied, and we will not be satisfied until justice rolls down like waters and righteousness like a mighty stream.
>
> (*Martin Luther King, 'I Have a Dream'*)

Politeness and formality

These modal auxiliary verbs also function to indicate degrees of politeness and formality. For example,

Can you lend me five pounds?	(*direct, colloquial*)
Will you lend me five pounds?	(*direct*)
Could you lend me five pounds?	(*tentative, more polite and formal*)
Would you lend me five pounds?	(*tentative, more polite and formal*)
May I borrow five pounds?	(*more formal and polite*)
Might I borrow five pounds?	(*tentative, polite and formal*)

Necessity–obligation

As well as indicating degrees of possibility and politeness, some modal auxiliary verbs express degrees of necessity or obligation. The writer or speaker can convey their attitude in ways that range from tentative suggestions to firm instructions. For example,

You _might_ try alternative therapies.	(*tentative suggestion*)
You _should_ try alternative therapies.	(*advice*)
You _ought_ to try alternative therapies.	(*firmer advice*)

You _need_ to try alternative therapies. (definite suggestion)
You _have_ to try alternative therapies. (definite instruction)
You _must_ try alternative therapies. (perhaps even more direct?)

It is important to recognise the use of modal verbs and phrases, as their function is to convey the speaker's – or writer's – attitude to the event referred to by the main verb. These auxiliary verbs allow speakers and writers to speculate and hypothesise, as well as to relate actual events. There are also modal phrases, which indicate degrees of possibility and certainty:

perhaps, maybe, surely, I suppose/think/guess

Activity 8.7

- Identify the modal auxiliary verbs used in the following extracts.
- How does this affect the meanings conveyed?
- What other modal phrases indicate degrees of possibility and certainty?

> **Extract 1**
>
> _Danny didn't want to say. He looked kind of shifty, nervous. I guessed I couldn't blame him after my outburst last night. So I promised myself I wouldn't explode again. I told myself that whatever the problem was we could work it out. Maybe we had to pay to play there? I'd heard bands had to do that sometimes. Or maybe he was changing the date until after Christmas? Which would be disappointing admittedly, but not disastrous._
>
> (Keith Gray, Happy)

> **Extract 2**
>
> _At midnight the solitary guard leaning in the shadows looked up at the conjoining planets and wondered idly what change in his fortunes they might herald._
>
> (Terry Pratchett, The Colour of Magic)

Implied meanings

The modal auxiliary verb 'would' can convey different meanings. It can be used in a straightforward way to convey past events, with the added suggestion that they are regular actions. This provides a way for pupils to vary their use of tenses in writing about the past.

> **Year 9:** recognise layers of meaning in the writer's choice of words, e.g. implied meaning, different types or multiple meanings

This extract from a novel uses 'would' to convey a sense of exasperation that these events happened without fail.

The white miner <u>would pretend</u> to give the orders, but it knew that it <u>would be</u> the boss boy who really got the work done. But a stupid white miner – and there were plenty of those – <u>would drive</u> his team too hard. He <u>would shout</u> and hit the men if he thought they were not working quickly enough and this could be very dangerous.

(Alexander McCall Smith, The Ladies No. 1 Detective Agency)

This is an indicative use of the auxiliary verb, but the same verb 'would' can also be used to express hypothetical situations. In persuasive texts, the writer may slip from one use to another, disguising the fact that some comments are simply the writer's speculation.

In the extract in Activity 8.8, the detective writer Patricia Cornwell is giving her theory about the identity of Jack the Ripper. She begins with modal verbs and phrases, clearly indicating that this is conjecture, but moves into more definite statements, implying that certain events actually took place.

Activity 8.8

- Identify the modal verbs and phrases used for conjecture in the following extract.
- Which verb phrases are indicative? Do these refer to known events?
- What meanings are implied by the writer's use of different verb moods?

NB Walter Sickert and Whistler were artists. John Merrick was the so-called Elephant Man, whose extreme deformity made him the focus of a popular 'freak-show' in Victorian London.

> It is quite possible that at some point Sickert paid his twopence and took a peek at Merrick. Sickert was living in London in 1884 and engaged to be married. He was an apprentice to Whistler and knew the East End rag shops in the slums of Shoreditch and Petticoat Lane and would etch them in 1887. Sickert went where the master went. They wandered together. Sometimes Sickert wandered about the squalor on his own. The 'Elephant Man' was just the sort of cruel, degrading exhibition that Sickert would have found amusing, and perhaps for an instant, Merrick and Sickert were eye to eye. It would have been a scene replete with symbolism, for each was the other inside out.
>
> (Patricia Cornwell, Portrait of a Killer: Jack the Ripper Case Closed)

Verb voice

Key words

voice: active, passive

Language in use

'The whereabouts of Osama bin Laden is unknown.'

So what assumptions are in the sentence, 'The whereabouts of Osama bin Laden is unknown'? It assumes that at the moment anyone is reading the sentence, they do not know where bin Laden is. That's anyone alive in the world. The words 'unknown' and 'not known' have the sense of 'not known to any human anywhere', as in, say, 'there is no known cure for malaria'. Clearly, this didn't apply to bin Laden. Presumably, he knew where he was, along with a group of his followers.

So why do many of us read a sentence like that without instantly finding it odd or illogical? It was published in Western newspapers in the context of what Western security forces were intending to do in Afghanistan. No sentence stands entirely on its own. It is, if you like, always coloured by what's being said or written around it. So, hidden in the sentence, is a sense that was what being spoken about, was a Western point of view, i.e. 'bin Laden's whereabouts is unknown to the West.'

(Rosen, 'The Power of the Passive')

The final way of classifying verb phrases is by their **voice**. The distinction between the active and passive voice requires some explicit teaching. The form of the passive is quite complex and

> **Year 7:** use the active or the passive voice to suit purpose

acquired relatively late by children. Pupils should be able to use the passive voice in formal, impersonal situations.

But, the use of the passive is significant in other ways. The above extract (Rosen, 2002) provides some interesting points about the assumptions that may be embedded in the use of the passive.

Changes from active to passive

It is sometimes assumed that the passive is simply a more formal version of an active sentence, but conveying the same meaning.

> **Year 8:** identify the key alterations made to a text when it is changed from an informal to a formal text, e.g. use of passive verbs

A dog bit my brother.	*(active voice)*
My brother was bitten by a dog.	*(passive voice)*

The point of view or emphasis has changed. The norm is for verbs to be used in the **active voice**, emphasising the role of the 'agent' – the dog.

Such structures can be transformed into the **passive voice**, which places emphasis on the recipient of the action – the brother. The agent can be mentioned, as above, or omitted.

My brother was bitten.

Some passive constructions are common in everyday language.

I was born in Cairo.

It is interesting that the active version is never used to emphasise the agent – the mother – and the action.

? My mother bore me.

Active structures such as 'Mary begat Jesus' only occur in older texts.

Form

Non-native users of English find the structure of passive verb phrases tricky to learn. Activities such as the following will demonstrate pupils' intuitive ability to use passive constructions.

Activity 8.9

Rephrase the following sentences to avoid mentioning any person involved:

I have lost the book.
My friend borrowed my bag.
She left it on the bus.

Tests

The following activity can make the structure of passive verb phrases explicit, using the tests of insertion and deletion.

Activity 8.10

Identify the changes to the structure in these pairs of sentences.

- What auxiliary verbs are inserted?
- What changes are made to the form of the main verb?

> *Teenagers spend a lot of money.*
> *A lot of money is spent.*
>
> *You must not park your car here.*
> *Cars must not be parked here.*
>
> *We will issue dinner passes.*
> *Dinner passes will be issued.*
>
> *No one told us about it.*
> *We were not told about it.*
>
> *The people have elected a new government.*
> *A new government has been elected.*

Functions of passive verbs

The passive voice places emphasis on the action itself, or the recipient of the action, rather than the agent. Although it is commonly assumed that the passive voice is simply a marker of formality, this change of focus happens for various reasons and therefore has slightly different effects. Some of the functions of the passive are listed below with examples.

> **Year 9:** write with differing degrees of formality, relating vocabulary and grammar to context, e.g. using the active or passive voice

1 It is used in scientific reports, where the identity of the agent is not important:

> *The crystals <u>were heated</u> over a bunsen burner and sulphuric acid was added.*

2 It is used in news reports, where the identity of the agent is unknown:

> *Two million pounds <u>were stolen</u> in a post office robbery.*

3 However, it may also be used to avoid identifying the agent:

> *Six blacks <u>were shot</u> in Soweto. (by the police)*

4 Or to leave the claim unsubstantiated:

> *Archer <u>was regarded</u> as a hero.*

5 It is often used in academic genres and tends to convey a more detached tone:

> *It <u>was felt</u> that Wolsey had grown too powerful.*

6 However, this may also be considered a way of avoiding mention of the agent – the authority for the statement remains vague, and may simply be the opinion of the writer.

> *Jane Austen's style <u>is said</u> to be flowery.*

Activity 8.11

- Identify the use of passive verbs in the following texts.
- Why does the writer use the passive, rather than the active, voice?

> **Extract 1**
>
> RETURNING HOME after three weeks in Cornwall, we find various disasters. Nature had been following its own course while we'd been away. The vegetable patch, about whose success I have been crowing to anyone who would listen, had been damaged by storm and slug, those formidable enemies of the gardener. My runner bean canes had been blown over, crushing the peas next to them.
>
> (www.idler.co.uk/countrydiary)

Extract 2

Only after the last tree has been cut down. Only after the last river has been poisoned. Only after the last fish has been caught. Only then will you find that money cannot be eaten.

(Cree Indian prophecy)

Compound verb phrases

The previous examples in this section showed the various possible structures for a *single* main verb, but there is one further structure of verb phrases. It is very common, and is used intuitively.

Some verbs can combine with other main verbs to form a longer phrase. Some common examples are verbs expressing desires and intentions:

want	*I want to go/see/meet*
hope	*I hope to pass/succeed/save*
need	*I need to pay/leave/*
love	*I love to cook/read/run*
like	*I like to dance/write/travel*
stop	*I stop to listen/look/stare*

These all use the infinitive form – 'to' + verb – to combine the two main verbs. Some verbs are combined using the present participle:

enjoy   I enjoy dancing/reading/studying

Some verbs can use either structure:

like   I like to travel.   I like travelling.

In some cases, this changes the meaning:

stop   I stopped to listen.   I stopped listening.

These types of verbs can be combined into a longer string:

I expected to be able to enjoy relaxing.

In summary, in English, verb phrases take different forms to indicate various functions and meanings.

TABLE 8.1 Verb phrases summary

Form	The main verb can take suffixes '–s', '–ing', '–ed'.
	Primary auxiliary verbs can be used before the main verb: 'do', 'be', 'have'.
	Modal auxiliaries can also come before the main verb.

Functions	The verb phrase can express mood, voice, tense and aspect:			
	mood	indicative	imperative	subjunctive	conditional
	voice	active	passive		
	tense	present	past		
	aspect	continuous	perfect	continuous perfect	

Meanings	verb phrases convey subtle shades of meaning, relating to:
	time
	duration
	perspective
	degrees of possibility, necessity, obligation, politeness, formality

Clauses

This chapter moves up to the next level of grammar – the way phrases combine to form clauses.

TABLE 9.1 Levels of structure

One or more **morphemes**	combine to form	words.
One or more **words**	combine to form	phrases.
One or more **phrases**	combine to form	clauses.
One or more **clauses**	combine to form	sentences.
One or more **sentences**	combine to form	paragraphs and whole texts.

The five different types of phrase used in this chapter can be printed on individual cards. This allows pupils to experiment with the familiar tests of substitution, deletion, insertion and transposition in a physical way. The activities – which only take a few hours of group work – consolidate their understanding of phrase structure and demonstrate the seven types of clause.

This chapter on clause structure deals with *main* clauses. A main clause can stand alone, so in this sense this chapter explores the structure of simple sentences. This level of grammar provides the basis for study of more complex sentence structures in Chapter 10, which distinguishes between main and *subordinate* clauses.

A few key terms, such as 'Subject', 'Verb' and 'Adverbial', are introduced to describe the roles of phrases within clauses. (Capital letters are used to distinguish between the term 'verb' or 'adverb' to describe a word class, and the use of a similar term to describe the function of a phrase in clause structure.)

This explicit knowledge is applied to the study of poetry, showing how the usual structures may be rearranged for stylistic effect. It is also used to reinforce pupils' awareness of punctuation conventions – in particular, the use of full stops between main clauses.

What is a clause?

Language in use

I pull my hand away from her kitten, slowly. I step back.
  I can't leave.
  I'm losing the light. The shed gets darker. Shadows play tricks on my eyes. I manoeuvre the carrier into the drywall.
  I send her a telepathic thought. Please just go forward, and it will be all right. I sit in that shed a long time.
  She goes forward. I close the carrier door and she is finally, mercifully trapped.
  I take down the barricade. I triumphantly hand the box with the kittens to the neighbourhood caretaker. I am shattered. And I am humbled.
  I say a silent prayer, a plea for forgiveness, to this little one, the one that I missed.
                    (taken from Elizabeth Cava, Satsuma www.faunaoutreach.org/satsuma)

Clauses and sentences

It is rare to find texts that use mostly simple, one-clause sentences. Even stories for young children – and writing by young children – include longer sentences, combining more than one clause. However, the use of such simple structures can have some dramatic impact, as the above account of a cat rescue organisation shows.

The writer uses many **simple sentences**. This grammatical term needs some clarification. 'Simple' does not mean that the sentence is short, as the following examples show:

> *Please just go forward, and it will be all right.*
> *I triumphantly hand the box with the kittens to the neighbourhood caretaker.*

The longer example is a simple sentence, as it contains one clause. The first, shorter sentence combines two clauses with the conjunction 'and'. This leaves the question: What is a **clause**? The essential element of a clause is the Verb – each clause contains one verb phrase. If pupils can identify the verbs in the sentences above, they will see that the first sentence has two verb phrases: 'go' and 'will be', forming two separate clauses. The second sentence has only one verb; 'hand', so there is one clause.

A **main clause** is one that can stand alone. This explanation relies on an intuitive sense of grammatical structure; for example, the difference between the following two sentences:

Shadows play tricks on my eyes.
* Shadows playing tricks on my eyes...

The second sentence does not make complete sense. It suggests that something further is going to be added.

A more explicit definition of a main clause involves the concepts of finite vs non-finite verbs. This is explored in more detail in Chapter 10. **Finite verb** forms can stand alone, making complete grammatical sense:

I <u>pull</u> my hand away from her kitten. I <u>step</u> back.

Non-finite verb forms are the present and past participles, ending in '–ing' or '–ed'. They do not make complete grammatical sense.

<u>Pulling</u> my hand away from her kitten,...

Non-finite verbs can be used as connectives, linking a **subordinate clause** to a following main clause:

<u>Pulling</u> my hand away from her kitten, I <u>step</u> back.

The next section shows how phrases are combined to form various structures of clauses.

The seven patterns of clause structure

Key words
subject   verb: transitive, intransitive   object direct object   indirect object   complement   adverbial

There are seven basic clause structures in English. Six of these patterns are used in the short extract on page 123.

1. *I can't leave.*
2. *I step back.*
3. *I'm losing the light.*
4. *The shed gets darker.*
5. *I send her a telepathic thought.*
6. *Shadows play tricks on my eyes.*

A rephrasing of the sixth provides an example of the seventh.

7. *The shadows make me confused.*

The following activities explore these seven clause structures, using the tests of substitution, insertion, deletion and transposition. The elements of structure can best be demonstrated by activities that allow pupils to physically move the key elements around.

Make 24 cards from the following phrases. (The choice of phrases is inspired by the bizarre cartoons of Gary Larson, as they capture the imagination of pupils.) You could make the activities slightly easier by colour-coding each type of phrase.

Widow Twankey	*another alligator shoe*
an ageing beetle	*that band of head-hunters*
the politician	*one stale meat pasty*
irresistible	*most peculiar indeed*
dozed	*leapt*
tripped up	*should have placed*
wanted to hide	*was*
had abandoned	*skinned*
sent	*found*
with a broken spear	*on the porch*
in the hollow tree	*out of the blue*
before breakfast	*morosely*

Types of phrase

The first activity consolidates pupils' explicit understanding of different types of phrases.

Activity 9.1

Group the cards into types of phrase:

verb phrase	headword = verb
noun phrase	headword = noun
prepositional phrase	preposition introduces noun phrase
adverbial phrase	headword = adverb
adjectival phrase	headword = adjective

Combining phrases

NB Do not use *two* verb phrases for the following activities. For example, do not combine 'was' with another verb like 'tripped up', as this makes a single passive verb phrase. Also, do not combine 'found' with another verb like 'skinned', as this will make a complex sentence with a subordinate clause, introduced by a verb with the suffix '–ed':

> The politician <u>found</u> an ageing beetle <u>skinned</u> on the porch.

The next activity demonstrates pupils' intuitive understanding of clause structure.

Activity 9.2

Use the cards to make a variety of clauses (simple sentences).

- What is the smallest number of cards you need to make a grammatical structure?
- What is the largest number of cards you can combine into a grammatical structure?

Clause type 1

The next activity looks at the most simple clause structure in English grammar, using the minimum number of two phrases.

Activity 9.3

- Make a clause with only two cards. When you are satisfied that it makes complete sense, write it down as Example 1.
- Look at this type of clause structure:
  - What sort of phrase goes in the first position?
  - What sort of phrase comes second?
  - How many other cards can replace this second card?
- What are the terms for these two elements?

Applications to style

Year 8: explore the impact of a variety of sentence structures, e.g. recognising when it is effective to use short direct sentences

This simple **Subject** + **Verb** structure of a clause conveys the minimum information: the agent and the action. The clause can be formed from two words, or a more complex noun phrase and verb phrase.

Subject	*Verb*
Era	*ends.*
An era	*has ended.*
The Mode Daily Sweepstakes	*has ended.*
Email service from libraryreference.com	*is going to end.*

This structure tends to be used for dramatic impact, making a brief assertion that is later developed or explained.

The woman/wept.
No one/spoke.

Research into pupils' writing at GCSE shows that the occasional use of such simple sentences is a feature of A-grade performance. Lower grades tend to lack this confident variety of sentence structures, using a sequence of longer sentences.

Transitive vs intransitive verbs

This simple clause structure with a Subject and Verb is only possible with **intransitive** verbs. This term is used for verbs that can stand alone. In contrast, transitive verbs require another element to make complete sense. The following **transitive** verbs cannot be used in this simple structure: 'was', 'had abandoned', 'should have placed', 'skinned', 'sent', 'found'.

> * The politician sent ...

Some verbs can be used in either a transitive or intransitive sense – 'tripped up', 'wanted to hide':

> The politician wanted to hide an ageing beetle.   (transitive)
> The politician wanted to hide.   (intransitive)

This distinction is understood intuitively, so does not need to be explained for pupils' own language use. It can, however, be used to comment on the ways meanings may be implied in texts.

For example, in popular romantic fiction the female character tends to be associated with intransitive verbs – 'she breathed/smiled/sighed', etc. – whereas transitive verbs occur more often with the male character's actions – 'he kissed her/took her in his arms'. This may suggest that the male character has more impact on the world around him.

The linguist Norman Fairclough (1966) notes the choice of intransitive verbs in government statements, such as 'Weak teachers will go'. Rather than expressing this as an action on the part of the authorities – 'We will sack weak teachers' – the choice of an intransitive verb suggests that these teachers will simply disappear of their own accord!

Clause type 2

The next activity builds on this basic structure of Subject + Verb, by inserting a third element (**Adverbial**).

Activity 9.4

- Use one of the intransitive verbs, 'dozed' or 'leapt'.
- Choose a Subject.
- Add on a third card, so that the clause makes sense.
- Write the whole clause as Example 2 and label the first two parts.
- Answer these questions about the third part of the clause:
  - Which other cards can be used in the third place? (substitution)
  - What type of phrase are they?
  - What sort of extra information do they give about the Verb?
  - Can these phrases be moved to another position in the structure? (transposition)

Application to style

This SVA structure of clauses is very common. It occurs in all types of language use. (The previous sentence uses this structure.) The noun phrase and adverbial phrase can be expanded into more complex structures, but the basic clause structure remains simple. The following examples are taken from poetry and academic writing.

S	V	A
He	*collapses*	*like a balloon*
Dragon-lovers with sweet serious eyes	*brood*	*in a desert wood thick with bluebells*
		(Ted Hughes, 'Moon-Whales')

The long light	*shakes*	*across the lakes, (and)*
the wild cataract	*leaps*	*in glory.*
The splendour	*falls*	*on castle walls*
		(Tennyson, 'The Princess')

This basic SVA structure can be varied for stylistic effect. Pupils should be aware that the position of the adverbial phrase is flexible. In imaginative forms of writing, such as poetry, the Adverbial may be placed at the beginning of the structure for emphasis, or rhythmic effect:

A	S	V
Full fathom five	*thy father*	*lies*
		(Shakespeare, The Tempest*)*

Under a pool of streetlights	*the boy*	*stops.*
		(Hathorn and Rogers, 1994)

Occasionally, the order of Subject and Verb can be changed:

A	V	S
In every moon-mirror	*lurks*	*a danger.*

This basic structure is also found in formal, academic writing:

S	V	A
A wide variety of animals	*deceive*	*intermittently.*

The simple sentence may seem more complex, if the adverbial phrase is expanded for more precise detail.

S	V	A
A few unfortunates	*suffer*	*from a puzzling deficit, an inability to understand another's point of view.*
		(Aitchison, 1996)

Clause type 3

There are other types of clause structure that use three phrases. The next activity illustrates the function of the third element (**Object**) following transitive verbs.

Activity 9.5

- Use one of the verbs 'skinned' or 'had abandoned'.
- Choose a Subject. (You will see that the clause does not make complete sense yet.)
- Add on a third card.
- Write the whole clause as Example 3.
- Answer these questions:
  - Which other cards can be used in this third place? (substitution)
  - What type of phrase are they?
  - Are they the same ones that you could use as the Subject? (transposition)
  - What is their relationship to the Subject and Verb?
  - What other Verbs could you put in this structure? (substitution)

Application to style

This is the most simple clause structure using transitive verbs: a Subject followed by a Verb and an Object. Each of the phrases can be a single word, or expanded into more complex phrases.

S	V	O
I	*'ve known*	*rivers.*
I	*'ve known*	*rivers ancient as the world and older than the flow of human blood in human veins.*

(Langston Hughes, 'The Negro Speaks of Rivers')

Poetry provides examples of unusual clause structures, even reversing Subject and Object, for emphasis, or rhythmic effect:

O	A	A	S	V
a damsel with a dulcimer	*in a vision*	*once*	*I*	*saw.*

(Coleridge, Khubla Khan)

Formal, academic writing also uses this basic clause structure in simple sentences:

S	V	O
True deceit	*involves*	*'tactical deception'.*

But the use of simple sentences often seems more complex, because the noun phrases are expanded.

S	V	O
Possibly only one primate branch, the great apes,	*has*	*a true theory of mind, the ability to attribute intentions to others.*

(Aitchison, 1996)

Clause type 4

There is another clause structure using three elements. The verb 'to be' is the most commonly used verb, but operates in different ways. Its function is 'stative', rather than 'dynamic', as it expresses a state, or condition. Other verbs that share this function are 'appear', 'seem', 'look', 'sound', etc. The next activity explores the function of stative verbs, using 'was' to construct clauses (simple sentences).

Activity 9.6

- Use the verb 'was' to form a clause structure with three elements.
  - Write an equals sign (=) on the back of the card.
  - Discard all the prepositional phrases – you have already seen that these function as Adverbials.
- Choose a Subject.
- Add a third card – NOT a prepositional phrase.
- Write the clause down as Example 4.
  - What other cards can be used in this third position? (substitution)
  - What types of phrases are they?
  - If you turn over the 'was' card, does the sign '=' convey a similar meaning?
  - Can you swap these third cards round with the Subject? (transposition)
  - What happens to the meaning?
  - What happens to the style?
- Does this third element function in the same way as an object?
  - Compare the following two clauses.
  - Do you agree that they look like the same structure on the surface?
  - How many people are there in the first example? In the second example?

S	V	O
The politician	*tripped up*	*Widow Twankey.*

S	V	?
The politician	*was*	*Widow Twankey.*

Application to style

The SVC (Subject, Verb, **Complement**) structure is common in all types of language use. The following examples are taken from poems and academic writing.

S	V	C
some people	*are*	*flower lovers.*
I	*'m*	*a weed lover. (Nicholson, 'Weeds')*
The gesture theory	*is*	*an old one. (Aitchison, 1996)*

The noun and adjectival phrases may be simple, or expanded into more complex phrases.

> *Nasturtiums on earth/are/small and seething with horrible green caterpillars. (Ted Hughes, 'Moon-Whales')*

> *This property of displacement/is/one of language's most valuable characteristics. (Aitchison, 1996)*

Although it is grammatically possible to transpose the Subject, Verb and Complement, this stylistic variation tends to occur in imaginative writing. The unusual word order places emphasis on the quality of the Subject.

C	V	S
All mimsy	*were*	*the borrogroves. (Carroll, 'The Jabberwocky')*
Marvellously white	*is*	*the moon-lily. (Hughes, 'Moon-Whales')*

The adjectival phrase can be expanded:

> *Broad, soft, silent and white and like a huge barn-owl's/is/their flight. (Hughes, 'Moon-Whales')*

The Subject can also be expanded by adding an extra phrase at the end:

> *Such a peculiar lot/we/are, we people without money. (James Berry, 'Fantasy of an African Boy')*

Clause type 5

So far, we have seen three possible clause structures with three elements: the obligatory Subject and Verb may be followed by an Adverbial, an Object or a Complement. The next activity looks at clause structures with four elements Subject, Verb, Object, Complement.

Activity 9.7

- Use the Verb 'found'.
- Choose a Subject.
- Add another noun phrase for the Object.

- Although this should make complete sense, add one of the two adjective phrases.
- Write it down as Example 5.
- Answer these questions:
  - What happens to the meaning of the verb when you add this fourth card?
  - Could you put an equals sign (=) between any two cards? Or the verb 'was'?
  - Label the first three elements.
  - What function does this fourth element have: Adverbial, Object, Complement?

Application to style

This structure is comparatively rare in language use, as it occurs with a limited number of verbs. Even when such verbs are used, writers often prefer to make the structure explicit by inserting the verb 'to be'.

The market manager thought it [was] a serious matter.

Clause type 6

The next activity shows another clause structure using four elements.

Activity 9.8

- Use the Verbs 'found' or 'sent'.
- Use only noun phrases for the other three parts.
- Choose a Subject.
- Add two other noun phrases after the Verb, so that the clause makes sense.
- Write it down as Example 6.
- Answer these questions.
  - Can you rearrange and rephrase this clause, so that it means the same?
  - Which is the direct Object of the Verb? (What did the Subject actually find or send?)

Application to style

In languages such as German, there are two separate 'cases' (noun suffixes) for **direct** and **indirect objects**. As there are no such suffixes to indicate the role of nouns in English, the indirect object is often made more explicit by rephrasing the sentence. For example,

The manager wrote Mr Hook a letter.
That very day the market manager wrote a letter to Mr Hook.

Clause type 7

The previous six structures form the basis of most clauses in English grammar. However, there are a few verbs that require an **Adverbial** after the Object.

S	V	O	A
I	*pull*	*my hand*	*away.*
Shadows	*play*	*tricks*	*on my eyes.*
She	*left*	*her money*	*beside the chair.*

Activity 9.9

- Use the verb 'should have placed'.
- Choose Subject and an Object. (You will notice that the clause does not make complete sense.)
- Add a fourth card.
- Write it down as Example 7.
- Answer these questions:
  - What other cards can you use in this position? (substitution)
  - What information do they provide?
  - Label the fourth element.

Expanding basic clause structures

Apart from a few verbs, adverbial phrases are generally optional extras, providing more information about the time, place or manner of the event. Prepositional and adverbial phrases are very flexible, allowing many variations to the basic structure of clauses:

- More than one adverbial phrase can be inserted.
- Adverbial phrases can be placed in various positions in the structure.

In Activity 9.2, pupils expanded the clause, by adding as many Adverbials as possible. The next activity makes this intuitive awareness explicit.

Activity 9.10

- How many phrases can be used in a single clause?
- Expand a basic clause structure by adding phrases. (insertion)
- What type of phrases can be added?
- Can you move these phrases to other positions? (transposition)
- What is the function of these phrases?

Application to style

The following examples are taken from the account of a cat rescue operation provided at the beginning of the chapter (see page 123). They show the flexibility possible in the use of adverbial phrases.

Adverbial phrases are commonly placed at the end of clauses, providing more detail about the event: how, when and where?

> I/pull/my hand/*away from her kitten,*/*slowly*.

It is possible to use three adverbials, without 'cluttering' the structure of the clause.

> She gazes/*down at us*/*serenely*/*from her safe haven*.

Stylistic variation is possible with the position of Adverbials. Single words are commonly transposed, and moved to the beginning of the structure for emphasis.

> *Slowly* I pull my hand away from the kitten.
> *Serenely* she gazes down at us from her safe haven.

It is less common to place a phrase at the beginning of the structure, but it can be done for emphasis. In this case, a comma is normally used to separate the phrase from the Subject.

> *From her safe haven*, she gazes down at us serenely.

Adverbials – generally single words – can also be placed before or after the verb.

> I *triumphantly* hand the box with the kittens to the neighbourhood caretaker.
> It is *always* the one I missed.

Activity 9.11

- Identify the adverbial phrases in the following extract.
- Change the position of these phrases. (transposition)
- What is the effect of the original structure?

> **Silver**
>
> Slowly, silently, now the moon
> Walks the night in her silver shoon;
> This way and that, she peers, and sees
> Silver fruit upon silver trees;
>
> *(Walter de la Mare)*

Applications to punctuation

A common error in punctuation is the use of a 'comma-splice' rather than a full stop. This usually happens when pupils use short, one-clause sentences. It may be because they associate the use of full stops with pauses for breath. It is more reliable to see punctuation as marking grammatical divisions. Thus, the full stop divides complete clauses – simple sentences. The easiest way to recognise a clause is to identify verbs, as they are the essential element of any clause.

The following example of a 'comma-splice' shows two verbs in two separate clauses.

> I _started to peer_ around the garden, I _noticed_ Jim Boulder's car outside their garage.

Commas may be used before connectives to separate a subordinate clause, or to separate phrases within the clause.

> The robbers aren't going to come through the entrance, _so_ they would go through the back.
> _Behind the hedge_, I thought I saw a movement.

Activity 9.12

- Identify the verbs and any conjunctions in the following extract.
- Replace commas with full stops to separate complete clauses.

> _After a cup of tea and a biscuit I got to work, I started to see if they had forced their way in. The room was very stuffy, so I thought I would open the window, the view was of the back garden leading into woods. On my travels to the back of the house I bumped into Mrs Hinton she stopped to talk, on the other hand I could ask her a few questions, so here we are talking away._

Applications to style

Pupils may be reluctant to signal their use of simple, one-clause sentences with a clear full stop if they believe that good writing is characterised by long, complex sentences. They should notice how effective short sentences can be, by looking at examples such as the following.

This is an account by George Orwell. His prose style is a good example of his principles for writing. He believed that 'the great enemy of clear language is insincerity'. His style is strong and economical, using a number of effective, short, simple sentences. He also uses simple co-ordinating conjunctions: 'but' and 'and'.

Activity 9.13

Note the simple, one-clause sentences used in this account.

> *At last, after what seemed a long time – it might have been five seconds, I dare say – he sagged flabbily to his knees. His mouth slobbered. An enormous senility seemed to have settled upon him. One could have imagined him thousands of years old. I fired again into the same spot. At the second shot he did not collapse but climbed with desperate slowness to his feet and stood weakly upright, with legs sagging and head drooping. I fired a third time. That was the shot that did for him. You could see the agony of it jolt his whole body and knock the last remnant of strength from his legs. But in falling he seemed for a moment to rise, for as his hind legs collapsed beneath him he seemed to tower upwards like a huge rock toppling, his trunk reaching skyward like a tree. He trumpeted, for the first and only time. And then down he came, his belly towards me, with a crash that seemed to shake the ground even where I lay.*
>
> *I got up. The Burmans were already racing past me across the mud. It was obvious that the elephant would never rise again, but he was not dead. He was breathing very rhythmically with long rattling gasps, his great mound of a side painfully raising and falling. His mouth was wide open – I could see far down into caverns of pale pink throat. I waited a long time for him to die, but his breathing did not weaken. Finally I fired my two remaining shots into the spot where I thought his heart must be. The thick blood welled out of him like red velvet, but still he did not die. His body did not even jerk when the shots hit him, the tortured breathing continued without a pause. He was dying, very slowly and in great agony, but in some world remote from me where not even a bullet could damage him further.*
>
> (George Orwell, 'Shooting an Elephant')

Summary clause structure

There are seven basic clause structures in English:

- Subject + Verb
- Subject + Verb + Adverbial
- Subject + Verb + Object
- Subject + Verb + Complement
- Subject + Verb + Object + Complement
- Subject + Verb + indirect Object + direct Object
- Subject + Verb + Object + Adverbial

Clauses are formed by combining phrases. The essential element of any clause is the Verb. This chapter looked at main clauses – or simple sentences – which also have a noun phrase as Subject. Other clause structures are formed by adding phrases as an Object, Complement or Adverbial.

I/can't leave.	$S + V$
I/step/back.	$S + V + A$

I/'m losing/the light.	$S + V + O$
The shed/gets/darker.	$S + V + C$
The shadows/make/me/confused.	$S + V + O + C$
I/send/her/a telepathic thought.	$S + V + Oi + Od$
Shadows/play/tricks/on my eyes.	$S + V + O + A$

The usual order in English grammar is to begin with the Subject and Verb, but this pattern can be varied for stylistic effect. The most flexible element of clause structure is the Adverbial – either an adverbial or prepositional phrase. These are normally optional elements: more than one can be added in a variety of positions in the structure.

The next chapter looks at the ways clauses are combined to form a variety of sentence structures.

10

Sentences

This chapter moves to the highest level of grammar – the structure of sentences from clauses.

TABLE 10.1 Levels of structure

One or more **morphemes**	combine to form	words.
One or more **words**	combine to form	phrases.
One or more **phrases**	combine to form	clauses.
One or more **clauses**	combine to form	sentences.
One or more **sentences**	combine to form	paragraphs and whole texts.

This is as far as the study of grammar, or syntax, can take us. The organisation of paragraphs and the structure of different genres of texts is examined in Chapters 13 and 14.

Sentences can be classified in two ways: according to their *function* – to make statements, ask questions, give commands – as well as their *structure* – simple, compound or complex. This chapter builds on the awareness of simple sentences formed from one clause, introduced in the previous chapter. The familiar tests of insertion and deletion demonstrate ways in which compound and complex sentences are formed. Different types of connective are introduced, explaining the key terms: 'conjunctions', 'non-finite verbs' and 'subordinate clauses'. The test of deletion is used to clarify the difference between main and subordinate clauses and to explain the use of commas within sentences. The transposition test is used to demonstrate the ways that subordinate clauses can be moved for emphasis.

This technical understanding is applied to use of appropriate styles in writing. The effects on style of using various types and combinations of sentence structure are explored, using examples of writing for different purposes and audiences.

Functions of sentences

This section introduces one useful way of classifying sentences – by their function. The informal terms 'statement', 'question', 'command' can be used, but the technical terms are introduced for more precision.

Key words
declarative   interrogative   imperative   exclamatory

Language in use

Wouldn't it be great to . . .
Learn the Magic Words and Phrases to gain the Advantage in any Verbal Encounter!
Have you ever noticed that it's the best talkers, the ones able to win in a verbal wrestling match, that gain the success, the promotions, the extra sales, the popularity and the position of authority we would all like?
Now . . . never again find yourself at a loss for words
Now . . . never again come off second best in any verbal encounter
Now . . . never again wish that you had spoken up, made your point more strongly or stopped someone else's bad behaviour.
In this special report you will meet one of the world's leading authorities on personal communication and discover the secrets of CONVERSATION POWER. Plus you are invited to try his methods.
FREE FOR 30 DAYS.

(advertising leaflet, prepared by Vic Conant, president of Nightingale Conant)

The text above uses three different functions of sentences to achieve its persuasive purpose. It addresses the reader directly by asking questions at the beginning, before suggesting actions and then providing information in statements. It does not actually use the fourth function – an **exclamatory** sentence – but an exclamation mark follows one of the questions. These four functions of sentences will be explained below, using the accepted terminology for the different structures.

Making statements

The norm for writing is **declarative** sentences, often used to make statements. In this structure, the subject comes before the verb (underlined):

> *In this special report <u>you will meet</u> one of the world's leading authorities . . .*
> *Plus <u>you are invited to try</u> his methods.*

Asking questions

In English grammar, **interrogatives** are formed by moving the verb before the subject. This is straightforward for most verb phrases. If there is an auxiliary verb, this is moved before the subject:

> _Wouldn't it be great to Learn the Magic Words ...!_
> _Have you ever noticed ...?_

Interrogatives are easily recognised by the use of question marks – even though the first example actually uses an exclamation mark.

NB As Chapter 8 showed, the auxiliary verb 'to do' is used to form questions in the present and past tense. As it has no other function in such structures, it is sometimes called the 'dummy do'.

> _Do you like shopping?_
> _Did you always enjoy shopping?_

Giving instructions

Imperative sentences, used to express instructions, commands or suggestions, use the simple form of the infinitive, often with the verb 'to do' for negatives.

> _Go to the shops._
> _Don't take the bus._

The advertising leaflet above uses imperatives such as:

> _find yourself at a loss for words_

The negative word 'never' is used instead of 'don't'.

> _never ... come off second best in any verbal encounter_

Often imperatives are 'softened' by the use of modal verbs such as 'must', 'ought to': or 'should'

> _You should go to the shops._
> _You mustn't take the bus._

Making exclamations

Exclamatory structures are comparatively rare in spoken and written English, although the exclamation mark is often used to emphasise statements. Strictly speaking, exclamatory sentences are formed by the use of 'how' or 'what'. They differ from interrogatives, as the subject plus verb order remains.

> _How I love shopping!_
> _What a pleasure it is!_

Pupils should be aware that exclamation marks are often overused, conveying a very personal, excitable tone that is rarely appropriate in writing. The use of multiple exclamation marks should be reserved for communication between friends.

Applications to style

The use of interrogatives and imperatives in texts conveys a sense of personal interaction between writer and reader, or speaker and listener. Although this is not appropriate for texts, (such as essays), with an impersonal tone, addressing the reader directly can be effective in persuasive or instructional writing. Even in such texts, it is important to use these colloquial features with control.

> **Year 7:** recognise how writers' language choices can enhance meaning, e.g. variation in sentence structure

> **Year 7:** vary the structure of sentences within paragraphs to lend pace, variety and emphasis

---

Activity 10.1

- What sentence types are used in the following text?
- What does this reveal about the purposes of the text?
- What revisions could be made to improve this text?

> **BULLIED? STOP IT!**
>
> *I was once bullied. Horrible isn't it? I was once punched regularly. Horrible isn't it? I was once made to feel scared and alone. Horrible isn't it? I once told my teacher – it stopped. Wouldn't that be great?*
>
> *Bullies are cowards. They pick on you because they're jealous. They pick on you because they don't think you'll snitch.*
>
> *You can do something about it. You can stop them bullying you. You must tell your teacher. Or you can let them continue making your life hell. What will you do?*
>
> *What can I do to stop them?*
>
> *Firstly you must tell a teacher. They are trained to deal with bullies and despite what you may have heard, teachers do care.*
>
> *Secondly you must try and avoid being alone around the bullies. Cowards never pick on people if they are in groups.*
>
> *(student work)*

Sentence structures

The other way of classifying types of sentences is by the complexity of their structure – simple, compound or complex. This distinction is useful for teachers, as these terms are used in the mark scheme for SATs to distinguish between levels of achievement at Key Stage 3. For example, pupils who use mainly simple and compound sentences are assessed at the lowest level. Those who use some complex sentences with conjunctions such as 'because' achieve a slightly higher level. The use of a variety of sentence structures, including 'embedded' clauses and 'fronted' clauses for emphasis, is a marker of the highest level of achievement.

Key word
simple sentence

Language in use

In summertime village cricket is a delight to everyone. Nearly every village has its own cricket field where the young men play and the old men watch. In the village of Lintz in the County of Durham they have their own ground, where they have played these last 70 years. They tend it well. The wicket area is well rolled and mown. The outfield is kept short. It has a good clubhouse for the players and seats for the onlookers. The village team plays there on Saturdays and Sundays. They belong to a league, competing with the neighbouring villages. On other evenings they practise while the light lasts. Yet now after these 70 years a judge of the High Court has ordered that they must not play anymore. He has issued an injunction to stop them. He has done it at the instance of a newcomer who is no lover of cricket.

(Lord Denning, Law Report *Miller v Jackson, 1977)*

Use of simple sentences

The High Court judge Lord Denning was noted for his clarity of expression in legal reports – a genre usually characterised by its complex style. The extract above uses everyday vocabulary in a number of simple sentence structures.

A **simple sentence** consists of a single clause, i.e. containing one main verb.

> *In summertime village cricket is a delight to everyone.*
> *They tend it well.*
> *The wicket area is well rolled and mown.*
> *The outfield is kept short.*
> *It has a good clubhouse for the players and seats for the onlookers.*
> *The village team plays there on Saturdays and Sundays.*
> *He has issued an injunction to stop them.*

A simple sentence is not necessarily a short sentence, as the above examples show. However, the following activity shows the use of sentences that are clearly 'simple' – a single main clause formed from relatively short phrases. This is a feature of texts that require simplicity above all – for example, when an author is writing for an audience of young children. The following activity uses an extract from a book for children aged between 5 and 8.

Activity 10.2

- Identify the verbs in each sentence.
- Which sentences are simple – one-clause – structures?

> *The boy leaps out into the road.*
>
> *There's a blare of horns, a screaming of tongues and tyres.*
>
> *But the cat with no name feels safe in the boy's jacket.*
>
> *'Ahhhh,' the boy called Shane yells as he dives through.*
>
> *They won't follow him here.*
>
> (Libby Hathorn, Way Home)

Application to style

Simple sentence structures can be effective in writing for certain audiences and purposes. There is a trend these days towards clarity in language use in public documents, with the Plain English Campaign promoting more simplicity in style in their advice documents and annual awards. The previous chapters provided examples of writers such as George Orwell and Ernest Hemingway, who are known for their use of an effectively simple style.

Year 8: explore the impact of a variety of sentence structures, e.g. recognise when it is effective to use short direct sentences

Although it is worth showing pupils how effective short, direct sentences can be, their position is significantly different from such established writers. The issue of competence and style in language use can be illustrated by the joke:

> *Q: What is the definition of good taste?*
> *A: Someone who knows how to play the accordion, but chooses not to.*

The reader can assume that experienced writers have a full repertoire of language strategies and have made an informed decision – they know how to use complex sentences, but have chosen not to. Pupils, on the other hand, are at the stage of developing their language skills, so should display their competence in using a range of sentence structures. Most language use combines two or more clauses into longer sentences. This can be done in two ways: by *linking* main clauses into a compound sentence, or by *embedding* one, or more, subordinate clauses within a complex sentence.

Compound sentences

The first way of creating longer sentence structures is relatively simple, and acquired by children at an early stage of language development. Two or more clauses are linked in a simple sequence. The overuse of this style of sentence is a common weakness in pupils' writing – more so than the use of simple sentences. An explicit awareness of the structure of compound sentences may help when revising their work.

compound sentence   co-ordinating conjunction
main clause

Language in use

Becky came round to ours last week, but I don't think she's going to be good enough to get into the lacrosse team, because she 's just on her computer all the time and she had the same trousers on that Marie's got, but they didn't look as good and anyway Marie got hers first. Marie keeps saying that she's a vegetarian, but I'm sure I saw a Peperami sticking out of her bag. Anyway my Dad says that vegetarians are stupid, because all they do is eat chips and cheese and then they have a heart attack. David's having a party but it's going to be really bad, because his Mum's going to make the food and everyone had food poisoning last time and I don't care anyway, because I'm going to be in Spain. David's going to Barcelona, but he's only going for ten days and we're going for two weeks and I've got my own room with a TV and everything.

(Neil Gaukwin, comedian and poet)

The example above is a parody of a young person's style of writing. The writer intuitively used long, mainly compound sentence structures to create a tone of excitable rambling, as one idea leads on to the next. The links between ideas are confined to simple addition – 'and' – or opposition – 'but' – with some expression of cause – 'because'.

A **compound sentence** links two or more clauses. The link may be a comma, separating each clause:

> And the cat with no name <u>sees</u> a flash of cruel teeth, <u>hears</u> the angry loud bark of the monster dog, <u>smells</u> the blood and the hunger and the danger.

It is more usual to link the clauses with a conjunction:

> David's having a party <u>but</u> it's going to be really bad.
> He's only going for ten days <u>and</u> we're going for two weeks.

Transposition test

There are only four conjunctions used to form compound sentences:

> *and, but, so, or*

Pupils could learn these as a list, but it is better to understand their role in structure. The term **co-ordinating conjunction** refers to their function: they operate as simple links, so their position is always *between* two clauses. The test of transposition can demonstrate this and therefore explain the different role of subordinating conjunctions, such as 'because'.

Activity 10.3

- Reverse the order of the two clauses in the following sentences.
- What happens to the position of the conjunction (underlined)?
  - *It is a sunny day <u>and</u> everyone is in the park.*
  - *I want to play football <u>but</u> there's a maths test tomorrow.*
  - *We can go shopping to Meadowhall <u>or</u> we can watch a video.*
  - *I didn't like the film <u>so</u> I left early.*
  - *I left early <u>because</u> I didn't like the film.*

Deletion test

The deletion test can be used to demonstrate the different roles of main and subordinate clauses. A **main clause** is one that can stand alone, making complete grammatical sense.

Activity 10.4

- Remove the conjunctions from the following sentence.
- Does each clause make grammatical sense?
- What do you need to insert in place of the conjunctions?

  David's going to Barcelona, but he's only going for ten days and we're going for two weeks and I've got my own room with a TV and everything.

Application to punctuation

The role of punctuation marks is to make the sentence structure clear for a reader. The accepted rule was that a comma is required before the conjunctions 'but', 'so' and 'or', but not needed before 'and'. These conventions are changing in contemporary language use. Some writers choose to use commas before 'and'; others no longer use commas before 'but', 'so' and 'or'.

There is some controversy about the use of co-ordinating conjunctions at the beginning of sentences. The familiar rule is:

You should not begin a sentence with <u>and</u> or <u>but</u>.

Pupils should be aware that these conjunctions function as linking words between clauses. Their occasional use at the beginning of a sentence should be a deliberate stylistic choice for emphasis. George Orwell, for example, uses this device:

Language in use

You could see the agony of it jolt his whole body and knock the last remnant of strength from his legs. <u>But</u> in falling he seemed for a moment to rise, for as his hind legs collapsed beneath him he seemed to tower upwards like a huge rock toppling, his trunk reaching skywards like a tree. He trumpeted, for the first and only time. <u>And</u> then down he came, his belly towards me, with a crash that seemed to shake the ground even where I lay.

(Orwell, 'Shooting an Elephant')

Application to style

Year 7: comment, using appropriate terminology on how writers convey setting, character and mood through word choice and sentence structure

Perhaps because the most simple way of linking sentences by 'and' is learned at an early stage by children, the repeated use of such compound sentences has become a marker of unsophisticated or childlike expression. The connective then is often used for a similar function. This style may be used deliberately to create an appropriate voice for a narrator, or character, in novels.

Activity 10.5

- Identify the use of simple co-ordinating connectives in the following passages.
- What does this suggest about the fictional characters in each extract?

Extract 1

Now you'd think, and I'd think, and everybody with a bit of imagination would think, that we'd done as clean a job as could ever be done, that with the baker's shop being at least a mile from where we lived, and with not a soul having seen us, and what with the fog and the fact that we weren't more than five minutes in the place, that the coppers should never have been able to trace us. But then, you'd be wrong, I'd be wrong and everybody else would be wrong, no matter how much imagination was diced out between us.

(Alan Sillitoe, The Loneliness of the Long Distance Runner)

Extract 2

Suddenly Lok understood that the man was holding the stick out to him but neither he nor Lok could reach across the river… The stick began to grow shorter at both ends. Then it shot to full length again.

  The dead tree by Lok's ear acquired a voice.

  'Clop!'

His ears twitched and he turned to the tree. By his face there had grown a twig: a twig that smelt of other, and of goose, and of the bitter berries that Lok's stomach told him he must not eat.

(Golding, The Inheritors)

Complex sentences

It is important for pupils to display competence in handling a variety of complex sentence structures. This section demonstrates the stylistic effects of complex sentences. It shows how pupils can identify subordinate clauses and use two ways of combining these with a main clause. It shows how the position of subordinate clauses can be varied for emphasis.

Key words

complex sentence   subordinate clause   subordinating conjunction
non-finite verb   relative clause   embedded clause   fronted clause   adverbial clause

Language in use

Do you like a long sentence that meanders towards the far-off full stop, travelling along the way through subordinate clauses that proliferate, then build up into lists, tropes, asides, tossed-off aperçus, always thickening the texture of the paragraph, which it inhabits entirely, and somehow re-enacting the complexity, the density of the experience?

Or do you like a short one?

The areas I have worked in – stand-up comedy, drama and journalism – do not encourage the lengthy, ornate thought. And the world we inhabit accelerates everything, so that every scene is shorter, every image quickly replaced by the next.

(Arthur Smith, Guardian)

As Arthur Smith comments in his article, 'ornate' sentence structures are used so rarely that the modern reader struggles to cope. The first sentence above is extremely complex, combining five (or more) clauses. In language use today, complex sentences are generally restricted to two or three clauses. This still allows the writer to express more complex relationships between the ideas in each clause.

A **complex sentence** combines a main clause with at least one **subordinate clause**. These subordinate clauses can be connected to the main clause in two ways:

- subordinating conjunctions   'since', 'while', 'that', 'whose', etc.
- non-finite verb forms   'travelling', 'thickening', 'reading', etc.

Transposition test

There are many **subordinating conjunctions**, such as:

> *because, since, although, while, if*

Although these conjunctions can be learned as a list, pupils can learn to recognise them by understanding their role in the structure.

The previous section showed how co-ordinating conjunctions – 'and', 'but', 'so', 'or' – function as simple *links*, always operating between two clauses. In contrast, the role of subordinating conjunctions is to *bind* a clause within the overall structure. The following activity uses the test of transposition to demonstrate the way that subordinating conjunctions are not free-standing links, but tightly bound to the clause they introduce.

Activity 10.6

- Transpose the order of clauses in the following sentences.
- What happens to the position of the conjunctions (underlined)?

> *Everyone is in the park, <u>and</u> the sun is shining.*
> *Everyone is in the park, <u>because</u> the sun is shining.*
>
> *I want to play football, <u>but</u> there is a maths test tomorrow.*
> *I want to play football, <u>unless</u> there is a maths test tomorrow.*
>
> *We can go shopping, <u>or</u> we can watch a video.*
> *We can go shopping, <u>unless</u> you prefer to watch a video.*

Deletion test

Subordinate clauses, unlike main clauses, cannot stand alone. The test of deletion can be used to identify subordinate clauses.

Activity 10.7

- Identify the subordinate clauses in the following sentences.
- Which clause can be deleted, leaving a complete simple sentence?

> *Because it is a sunny day, everyone is in the park.*
> *Even though it's a sunny day, no one is in the park.*
> *It was a sunny day, when everyone was in the park.*
>
> *I want to play football, unless there's a maths test tomorrow.*
> *Although I want to play football, there's a maths test tomorrow.*
> *Whenever I want to play football, there's a maths test the next day.*
>
> *We can go shopping to Meadowhall, unless we watch a video instead.*
> *If we go shopping to Meadowhall, we can watch a video later.*
> *After we go shopping to Meadowhall, we can watch a video later.*

Relative clauses

The subordinating conjunctions – 'who', 'whom', 'which', 'that' – are grouped together as they introduce a **relative clause**, giving more information about somebody or something. These clauses are often used within the structure of a noun phrase, rather than as a separate clause in the structure of the sentence. The term **embedded clause** refers to the complexity of this structure.

> He [, _whose_ design includes whatever language can express,] must often speak of what he does not understand.

> Do you like a long sentence [that _meanders towards the far-off full stop]_ ... ?

Application to punctuation

Commas are often used to make the boundary between clauses clear to a reader:

> The world we inhabit accelerates everything, _so that_ every scene is shorter.

Year 8: combine clauses into complex sentences, using the comma effectively as a boundary signpost

When a conjunction is used _between_ clauses, it can be argued that it is a clear structural signpost in itself and needs no further punctuation. Many contemporary writers omit commas in such cases. Orwell, for example, is not consistent, using a comma before 'but' in one sentence, and omitting it in another sentence in the same text.

> At the second shot he did not collapse _but_ climbed with desperate slowness to his feet and stood weakly upright ... It was obvious that the elephant would never rise again, _but_ he was not dead.

For some reason, it is the accepted convention that no comma is needed before the conjunction 'that', but required before the alternative choice of conjunction 'which'.

> I realised _that_ it was quite a while since I had read a novel _that_ is largely made up of massive, page-turning sentences.
> I had read a novel, _which_ is largely made up of massive, page-turning sentences.

However, a comma is a useful marker, always used when the subordinate clause comes at the beginning of the sentence:

> _When_ the mind is unchained from necessity, it will range after convenience.

Non-finite verbs as connectives

Clauses in a complex sentence can also be connected by non-finite verbs. A **non-finite verb** takes three forms:

TABLE 10.2 Non-finite verbs

verb + 'ing'	<u>Rushing</u> out of the house, I forgot to bring my library book.
verb + 'ed'	<u>Bored</u> by the assembly talk, most people stopped listening.
irregular past participle	<u>Driven</u> by ambition, she rose to the top of her profession.

These verb forms are called non-finite, as they are 'unfinished', in the sense that they do not make complete grammatical sense. This can be shown by a deletion test. When you remove the main clause, the remaining structure does not make complete sense:

> * *Rushing out of the house...*
> * *Bored by the assembly talk...*
> * *Driven by ambition...*

Like subordinating conjunctions, these connectives remain bound to the clause they introduce. The subordinate clause can be moved to other positions in the sentence structure:

> *Most people stopped listening, <u>bored</u> by the assembly talk.*
> *She rose to the top of her profession, <u>driven</u> by ambition.*

This type of complex sentence structure suggests that the two clauses, or events, are closely related in time. As pupils acquire this structure, they tend to overuse it. The following activity encourages pupils' awareness of this style, which is also a common feature of 'pulp' fiction.

Activity 10.8

- Identify the subordinate clauses in the following examples from romantic fiction.
- Underline the non-finite verb forms.
- Which clause can be deleted leaving a complete grammatical sentence?

> *She shifted in her seat, eyeing Sarah with interest.*
> *She waited, holding her breath without realising that she did so.*
> *In silence she did so, flicking the switch and filling the room with light.*
> *Outside she sat in the car for a moment, resting her head against the cold steering wheel.*
> *Alerted by sudden small gusts of wind, Deirdre Shackleton looked up.*
> *Shaken by the directness of words which re-echoed her own recent thoughts, Sarah was embarrassed.*
> *Smiling, Katie nodded.*
> *Scratching his head, the elderly locksmith stared at the back of the door.*
> *Squaring her shoulders, she pressed the bell with a resolute finger.*
> *Arriving home, her happiness turned to anger in a flash.*

Applications to style

Although the ability to use complex sentence structures is probably acquired gradually through reading a rich variety of texts, some explicit practice in combining sentences may be useful. Pupils can be asked to revise examples from their own writing.

Year 9: review and develop the meaning, clarity, organisation and impact of complex sentences in their own writing

The following activity provides one example, showing how a sequence of simple sentences may be combined into longer sentence structures. This allows the writer to emphasise particular clauses, by placing them at the beginning of the sentence. The term **fronted clause** is used for this stylistic device.

Activity 10.9

■ Combine these four simple sentences into one longer sentence in as many ways as possible. You can reorder, or rephrase, the clauses.

   I walked into the house. It was strangely quiet. I called out. No one was at home.

■ Note the types of connectives used – whether co-ordinating or subordinating.

■ Is the sentence compound, complex, or a mixture of the two?

■ Which clause has been emphasised, by placing it at the beginning of the sentence?

Adverbial clauses

Subordinate clauses are often referred to as **adverbial clauses**. This is because they function like adverbs or adverbial phrases in significant ways:

■ Their role is to add information to the main clause, such as how, when, where or why it happened.

■ Like adverbs, these clauses can be deleted or transposed to another position in the structure.

For example, the following clauses express why and when I called out. The brackets ([ ]) indicate that they can be deleted, leaving a complete grammatical structure.

   [Unnerved by the strange quiet] [as I walked into the house,] I called out, [fearing that no one was at home.]

The substitution test shows that subordinate clauses can often be replaced by an adverbial phrase, as this activity demonstrates.

Activity 10.10

Replace the subordinate clauses with a single word or phrase.

When the weather is fine, everyone is in the park.

Rushing out of the house, I forgot my library book.

As I walked through the door, I called out, fearing that no one was at home.

Application to language change

Year 8: recognise some of the differences in sentence structure, vocabulary and tone between a modern English text and a text from another historical period

The use of long, complex sentence structures is a common feature of texts from earlier historical periods. Because of this complexity, a variety of punctuation marks are needed as markers between the clauses.

Activity 10.11

- Note the number of clauses in this complex sentence, written in 1755.
- What connectives are used – subordinating conjunctions or non-finite verbs?
- What punctuation marks are used to mark boundaries between clauses?

> *Who will consider that no dictionary of a living tongue ever can be perfect, since, while it is hastening to publication, some words are budding, and some falling away; that a whole life cannot be spent upon syntax and etymology, and that even a whole life would not be sufficient; that he, whose design includes whatever language can express, must often speak of what he does not understand.*
>
> *(Samuel Johnson, Preface to the English Dictionary)*

Application to style

In some genres of writing, it may be appropriate for pupils to use compound sentence structures. A diary entry, for example, is a form of personal writing, where the writer may wish to convey a spontaneous, quasi-spoken voice. The dilemma for teachers, and pupils, is that such writing is still assessed for competence in handling a variety of sentence structures. The following text was written by a Year 7 pupil asked to produce a diary entry.

Activity 10.12

- Identify the use of co-ordinating conjunctions (compound sentence structures) in the following diary entry.
- Has the writer used subordinating conjunctions (complex sentence structures)?
- What advice would you give the pupil for redrafting this work?

> *1 January 2005*
>
> *Dear Diary*
>
> *Yesterday wasn't as good as I had hoped. The play was brilliant and the way everything worked and fitted together was extremely clever or at least that's what I thought.*
>
> *Thing is you see, we only watched the fireworks from our hotel windows, due to the fact that almost all of us were too tired so we tried to catch a ride on a bus but they all were out of business because of all the fireworks. Which ended up meaning that we had to walk almost all the way to the hotel, which was about two miles from where we had been waiting.*
>
> *There was one thing we hadn't planned which was really enjoyable and that was a salsa band and that was in the bar/restaurant we went into for a light snack.*
>
> *I guess overall it was quite annoying but still an enjoyable day; anyway I'm really tired now so I think it's time to rest.*
>
> *Goodnight.*
>
> *(child's diary)*

Application to reading

Awareness of sentence structures can also be applied to reading skills. Pupils should become aware of the ways that a writer's use of varied sentence structure contributes to effects created by vocabulary choice and sound effects.

> **Year 8:** comment, using appropriate terminology on how writers convey setting, character and mood through word choice and sentence structure

The final activity in this chapter uses an extract from a novel. It shows how pupils can use their grammatical knowledge to comment on stylistic effects. Sentence structure works together with vocabulary – the meanings and sound effects of words.

> **Year 8:** recognise how writers' language choices can enhance meaning, e.g. repetition, emotive vocabulary, varied sentence structure or line length, sound effects

See **Chapter 11** on phonology for further analysis of sound effects in language use.

See **Chapter 12** on semantics for the effects of figurative and emotive vocabulary.

Activity 10.13

These are the final paragraphs from a novel entitled *The Awakening* (1899).

- What impression does it convey of the setting, character and mood of the episode?
- Note the variety of sentence structures used, as well as vocabulary choice and sound effects.
- What effects are created by the use of these structures?

> *The water of the Gulf stretched out before her, gleaming with the million lights of the sun. The voice of the sea is seductive, never ceasing, whispering, clamouring, murmuring, inviting the soul to wander in abysses of solitude. All along the white beach, up and down, there was no living thing in sight. A bird with a broken wing was beating the air above, reeling, fluttering, circling disabled down, down to the water.*
>
> *Edna had found her old bathing suit still hanging, faded, upon its accustomed peg.*
>
> *She put it on, leaving her clothing in the bath-house. But when she was there beside the sea, absolutely alone, she cast the unpleasant pricking garments from her, and for the first time in her life she stood naked in the open air, at the mercy of the sun, the breeze that beat upon her, and the waves that invited her.*
>
> *How strange and how awful it seemed to stand naked under the sky! How delicious! She felt like some new-born creature, opening its eyes in a familiar world that it had never known.*
>
> *The foamy wavelets curled up to her white feet, and coiled like serpents about her ankles. She walked out. The water was chill, but she walked on. The water was deep, but she lifted her white body and reached out with a long, sweeping stroke. The touch of the sea is sensuous, enfolding the body in its soft, close embrace.*
>
> *She went on and on. She remembered the night she swam far out, and recalled the terror that seized her at the fear of being unable to regain the shore. She did not look back now, but went on and on, thinking of the bluegrass meadow that she had traversed when a little child, believing that it had no beginning and no end.*
>
> *(Kate Chopin, The Awakening)*

Summary sentence types

Sentences can be classified by their form and function:

declarative	*subject before verb*	*makes a statement*
interrogative	*verb before subject*	*asks a question*
imperative	*base form of verb*	*expresses a command*
exclamatory	*begins with 'what' or 'how'*	*expresses an exclamation*

Sentences can also be classified by their structure:

simple	*a single main clause*
compound	*two or more main clauses linked*
complex	*a main clause, combined with two or more subordinate clauses*

Clauses are classified into:

main	*can stand alone*	*finite verb form*
subordinate	*cannot stand alone*	*introduced by subordinating conjunction or non-finite verb form (ending in '–ing' or '–ed')*

Subordinate clauses can be identified by the familiar tests:

TABLE 10.3 Tests for subordinate clauses

Deletion	They can be deleted, leaving a complete grammatical structure.
Transposition	They can be moved to various positions in the structure.
Substitution	They can be replaced by adverbs or adverbial phrases.

Beyond grammar

11

Phonology

This chapter looks at the sounds used to form words in English. Although individual sounds do not have a meaning, there is clearly a shared emotional response to the effects of sounds. Pupils at Key Stages 3 and 4 should be aware of sounds and their effects. There are relatively few terms recommended in the Framework: 'vowel', 'consonant', 'alliteration', 'assonance', 'onomatopoeia'.

Pupils grasp these terms quickly and apply them to texts, but often make over-simple observations, such as:

There is alliteration that makes the line flow.

This type of comment suggests that the repetition of any sound conveys the same, rather vague, effect.

Year 7: experiment with the sound effects of language, including the use of alliteration, rhythm and rhyme

This chapter explores intuitive responses: some sounds are perceived as larger or more forceful; others seem softer or more attractive. An understanding of some key terms and concepts from phonology can help pupils comment more precisely on the effects of sounds in poetry and persuasive texts. Awareness of the ways that the sounds of language are produced in the mouth and throat makes the qualities of different types of sounds explicit.

Further concepts from phonology are introduced for teachers wishing to develop their own understanding. The term 'phoneme' is explained in a brief introductory section. The technical symbols from the International Phonetic Alphabet (IPA) will not be used. Instead, sounds will be represented informally by conventional spelling.

The chapter moves from the study of individual sounds to other features of spoken language: stress, rhythm and intonation. The study of metre in poetry has been covered in many other texts, so is only mentioned in passing. Some examples from the study of rhetoric are included to show the connection between grammatical structure and sound effects.

Sounds and letters

Key words

sounds   phonemes   vowel   consonant

Language in use

A moth is not a moth in mother,
Nor both in bother, broth, or brother,
And here is not a match for there,
Nor dear and fear for bear and pear,
And then there's doze and rose and lose –
Just look them up – and goose and choose,
And cork and work and card and ward
And font and front and word and sword,
And do and go and thwart and cart –
Come, I've hardly made a start!
A dreadful language? Man alive!

(author unknown)

This poem makes the important point about the English language that 'sounds and letters don't agree'. One important distinction is between consonants and vowels. Pupils will be familiar with these terms applied to the letters used in writing. However, it is important to be aware that the English alphabet does not correspond exactly to the number of **sounds** used in the language.

The 26 letters of the alphabet suggest that English uses 5 vowels and 21 consonants. There are, in fact 44 significant sounds – or **phonemes** – used in spoken English. There are 24 **consonant** phonemes, many of which correspond to a letter of the alphabet:

p, b, t, d, k, g, f, v, s, z, m, n, h, l, r, w

NB The 'k' phoneme can be represented by the letter 'k' or 'c' or 'ch'.

There are phonemic symbols to represent the remaining consonant sounds, but these can be illustrated using conventional spelling.

/ch/	*as in*	*'church'*
/dge/		*'judge'*
/sh/		*'sheep'*
/je/		*'leisure'* (this phoneme only occurs in the middle of English words)
/y/		*'yacht'*
/ng/		*'singing'* (this phoneme only occurs in the middle of English words)

/th/	'thy'	
/th/	'thigh'	(two phonemes are represented by the letters 'th')

There are 20 **vowel** phonemes used in the English language, but only five letters in the alphabet. This means that there are many unfamiliar symbols. This technical knowledge is not needed before A level or degree study. It is sufficient for pupils to be aware that there are more than 5 vowel sounds in English. The section on vowels uses conventional spellings to illustrate the qualities of vowel sounds and their effects.

Consonants

This section explores the emotional effects that certain consonant sounds convey, and introduces some terms from phonology to explain the physical basis for these effects.

Key words

onomatopoeia   consonant   plosive   fricative   nasal   voiced   unvoiced

Activity 11.1

> **Sounds U Like**
>
> In 1980 The Sunday Times ran a poll to find out the ten most popular words. They were:
>
> | 1 | gossamer | 6 | twilight |
> |---|----------|---|----------|
> | 2 | crystal | 7 | murmur |
> | 3 | autumn | 8 | caress |
> | 4 | peace | 9 | mellifluous |
> | 5 | tranquil | 10 | whisper |
>
> (www.thetimesonline.co.uk)

Why do people respond favourably to these words? Is it simply the meaning – many refer to delicate properties – or are we influenced by the sound effects as well?

- Say each word out loud and notice the consonant sounds.
- What sounds occur several times in these words?
- Are some sounds never, or rarely, used in these words?
- What does this tell us about sounds we prefer?

Sound effects

The previous activity relied on an impressionistic response to **consonant** sounds –
some are perceived as softer, or harder. These effects are used, not only in poetry,
but also in advertising. The sounds used to form words are arbitrary in many ways.
Although there are a few examples of **onomatopoeia** in any language – 'clash',
'murmur', 'miaow' – the relationship between sound and meaning is usually arbitrary – the sounds 'c', 'a' and 't' do not represent the type of animal named.

   Despite this, there is a sense in which 'sounds have meaning'. In the following
article, the choice of a brand name is influenced by the belief that 'most phonemes
have a distinct emotional character'.

Activity 11.2

- Read this article about the choice of name for a new piece of technology, the BlackBerry.
- What claims are made about the effects of certain sounds?
- Can you think of any other products with effective-sounding names?

> As soon as the naming gurus at Lexicon Branding Inc. saw the hand-held wireless prototype
> that Research In Motion Ltd. had produced, they were struck by the little keyboard buttons,
> which resembled nothing so much as seeds.
>   'Strawberry!' suggested one.
>   No, 'straw–' is a slowwwww syllable, said Stanford University linguist Will Leben, who also is
> director of linguistics at Lexicon, based in Palo Alto, Calif. That's just the opposite of the zippy
> connotation Research In Motion wanted. But '–berry' was good: Lexicon's research had shown
> that people associate the b sound with reliability, said David Placek, who founded the Palo Alto,
> Calif., firm and is its president, while the short e evokes speed. Another syllable with a b and a
> short vowel would nail it . . . and within seconds the Lexicon team had its fruit: BlackBerry.
>   'Most phonemes have a distinct emotional character,' says psycholinguist Cynthia Whissell of
> Laurentian University in Sudbury, Ontario. Or as Dr. Leben puts it, 'sounds have meaning. There
> is a relationship between speech sounds and emotions.'
>   But phonologically, according to Lexicon's research, respondents rate the b sound as most
> strongly suggesting relaxation. In other words, the two b's say that using this hand-held won't
> require a 200-page manual. The short vowels in the first two syllables lend crispness: pushing a
> few buttons will quickly accomplish your goal. The alliteration conveys light-heartedness, much
> as Kit-Kat does. The final y, says Dr. Whissell, who has no connection to any naming company,
> 'is very pleasant and friendly, which is why you often find it in nicknames.'
>
>   (Sharon Begley, Wall Street Journal, 26 August, 2002)

Sound symbolism

As well as the emotional effects mentioned above, there seems to be a relationship
between sounds and physical properties. The following activity is based on an
experiment devised by Kohler (1929).

Activity 11.3

- Draw two shapes: one rounded and the other angular.
- Use the invented words 'takete' and 'maluma' and assign one to each shape.

Application to vocabulary

Although the sound patterns of most words are not related to meaning, certain combinations of sounds occur in groups of words that seem related. For example, the following words all begin with the consonants 'sl':

> *slack, slouch, sludge, slime, slosh, slash, sloppy, slug, sluggard, slattern, slut, slang, sly, slither, slow, sloth, sleepy, sleet, slip, slipshod, slope, slit, slay, sleek, slant, slovenly, slab, slap, slough, slum, slump, slobber, slaver, slur, slog, slate*

According to the linguist Firth (1964), 'A group of words such as the above has a cumulative suggestive value that cannot be overlooked in any consideration of our habits of speech. All the above words are in varying degrees pejorative.'

Activity 11.4

- Use a dictionary to collect groups of words beginning with the following letters: 'gl', 'sn', 'wr'.
- Can you find any common meanings?
- Does this help you to guess the meaning of unfamiliar words?

For example, here are some words beginning with 'sw':

> *sweep, sway, swing, swirl, swerve, swoop, swish, switch, swat, swipe, swab*

All these words suggest a sideways movement. This might help to guess the meanings of words such as 'swivel' or 'swoon'.

Place and manner of articulation

Why do certain consonant sounds have emotional effects? All consonant sounds are produced by blocking, then releasing, the airflow from the mouth or nose, but there is variation in the way the sounds are produced. Some technical terms from phonology will be introduced to clarify these differences in sound quality. Adding a few details may help pupils to explain the effects created by sound in poetry or persuasive writing. Further technical aspects are included for teachers wishing to extend their own understanding.

Plosive sounds

The term **plosive** is used to refer to consonants that are made with 'an explosion of air'. If you say the following sounds, you will notice that they are made by releasing air abruptly from the mouth:

> *p, b*   *t, d*   *k, g*

These consonants have been grouped in pairs to indicate the place of articulation – the position in the mouth.

> *p, b*   *made by closing off the air supply at the lips*
> *t, d*   *made by placing the tongue behind the teeth*
> *k, g*   *made at the back of the mouth*

Pupils should move beyond observing alliteration – the repetition of consonant sounds – to noticing which sounds are repeated and commenting on the emotional effects. Because these plosive sounds come to a stop, they are often associated with emotions such as firmness or determination:

> *Tackling drugs to build a better Britain.*

Perhaps more significant for the effect of these sounds is the aspect of 'voice'. The two sounds in each pair are distinguished by the amount of 'voicing'. If you place your hand over your throat as you say each one, you should notice that the vocal cords vibrate for the **voiced** sounds: 'b', 'd', 'g'. In advertising, it is suggested that the effect of voiced consonants is more 'luxurious' (see Activity 11.2). However, there were few voiced plosive sounds in Activity 11.1.

In contrast, the sounds 'p', 't', 'k' are silent, or **unvoiced**. Activity 11.3 showed that the unvoiced sounds 't' and 'k' are associated with an angular shape. An interesting correspondence between sound and meaning is shown in the group of words derived from the root *peuk* ('prick'):

> *impugn, expunge, pugilist, pugilistic, pygmy, pungent, pounce, poignant, point, puncture, punctuate*

The unvoiced plosive sound 'p' is made by the lips and suggests an energetic movement.

Fricative sounds

The term **fricative** refers to the different way other consonants are produced. If you say the following sounds, you will notice that they are made by releasing the air in a 'trickle' from the mouth:

> *th, sh, s, z, f, v*

These sounds can also be grouped in pairs: produced in the same place in the mouth, but with one sound voiced and the other unvoiced. For example, note the difference between the sound in the following pairs of words:

unvoiced	*voiced*
thigh	*thy (two phonemes represented by the letters 'th')*
fear	*veer*
Sue	*zoo*
shack	*Jacques, or the middle sound in 'leisure'*

Repetition of the 's' or 'z' sound, in particular, is often described as 'sibilance':

> *There be moe wasps that buzz about his nose* (Henry VIII)

The emotional effect of the unvoiced sounds may be 'softer', with the voiced sounds more 'zippy'. This, perhaps, influenced the choice of brand names with a 'z' sound:

> *Prozac, Amazon*

Of course, the associated meanings of other words with the same sound contribute to the appeal. For example, the use of the voiced fricative in the brand name:

> *Viagra – vitality, vigorous, vital*

Nasal sounds

The term **nasal** refers to consonants produced by releasing air through the nose, rather than the mouth. There are three nasal consonant sounds. One sound only occurs at the end of syllables in English, and is represented by the combination 'ng', as in 'singing':

> *m, n, ng*

If you say these sounds, you will notice that they are voiced. This, and the nasal quality, produces a sonorous effect if a number are used in a text; for example, in these lines from a poem:

> *The moan of doves in immemorial elms, and murmuring of innumerable bees*
> *(Tennyson, 'The Princess: Come Down, O Maid')*

The remaining consonant sounds are made in various ways. They are often perceived as soft, or attractive, sounds. Many occurred in the 'favourite words' in Activity 11.1:

> *l, r, w, y*

Activity 11.3 showed that the sounds 'm' and 'l' in the word 'maluma' are associated with a rounded shape. The next activity shows the way these consonant sounds are used for effect in poetry.

Application to poetry

Pupils should be aware of alliteration – the marked repetition of sounds – and begin to make more precise comments about the effects of the *type* of sound used.

Activity 11.5

- Read the first verse of two poems by the war poet Wilfred Owen.
- Compare the sound effects used in these extracts.
- What type of consonant sounds recur in each.
- What effects do these sounds convey?

Extract 1

Dulce et Decorum Est

Bent double, like old beggars under sacks,

Knock-kneed, coughing like hags, we cursed through sludge,

Till on the haunting flares we turned our backs

And towards our distant rest began to trudge.

Men marched asleep. Many had lost their boots

But limped on, blood-shod. All went lame; all blind;

Drunk with fatigue; deaf even to the hoots

Of disappointed shells that dropped behind.

(Wilfred Owen, The War Poems)

Extract 2

Exposure

Our brains ache, in the merciless iced east winds that knive us . . .

Wearied we keep awake because the night is silent . . .

Low, drooping flares confuse our memory of the salient . . .

Worried by silence, sentries whisper, curious, nervous,

But nothing happens.

(Wilfred Owen, The War Poems)

Vowels

Whereas consonant sounds are made by blocking the flow of air, vowels are released from an open mouth. There are 20 vowel sounds in English. Some are short, while other vowel sounds are held for a longer time. The shape of the lips and position of the tongue also changes the sounds made. Although vowel sounds do not *mean* anything in isolation, they appear to convey certain qualities.

The following activity is based on an experiment devised by the linguist Edward Sapir (1970 [1929]):

Activity 11.6

- Imagine two tables, one large and one small.
- Which of these words – 'mil' or 'mal' – would you assign to each table?
- Can you explain your choice of word?

Sound symbolism

The previous activity showed that some vowel sounds are associated with physical qualities. Is it convincing to claim that vowel sounds have meaning, in the sense of emotional effects? The following article refers to research into the relative attractiveness of names. Pupils may like to apply these ideas to their own names.

Language in use

There is such a thing as a pretty name, some scientists believe, meaning it is good news if you are a Laura or Matt but not so great if you are called Paul and Anne.

Amy Perfors, at Massachusetts Institute of Technology, posted 24 pictures of men and women on a website called Hot or Not. People visiting the site were asked to vote on the attractiveness of the photographs. Every so often she changed the names beneath the pictures to see if it would affect how the votes fell.

She found that the men, when allotted first names such as Nick and Matt, where the stressed vowel is made at the front of the mouth, were voted more attractive than when they were given the name Paul or Charles – where the dominant vowel is made at the back of the throat.

She found it was the reverse for women. Those with names such as Jess and Anne were marked as less attractive than a Julie and Susan.

(Perfors, 2004)

This research suggests that certain vowel sounds have a more favourable effect than others, depending on whether the vowel sound is made at the front or back of the mouth. But for some reason the response differs according to gender. Perfors sums up her conclusions as follows:

- Males, whose names have a vowel sound made at the front of the mouth, are statistically more attractive:

    Dave, Craig, Ben, Jake, Rick, Steve, Matt

- Those whose name has a vowel sound made at the back of the mouth proved less attractive:

    Lou, Paul, Luke, Tom, Charles, George, John

- The opposite is true for females. Names with a back vowel proved more attractive:

    Laura, Julie, Robin, Susan, Holly, Carmen

- Female names with a front vowel had a less favourable response:

    Melanie, Jamie, Jess, Jill, Amy, Tracy, Ann, Liz

Short vs long vowel sounds

The 20 vowel sounds of English can be grouped in various ways. The example above concentrated on the place of articulation – whether it is at the front or back of the mouth. This aspect, however, is not as obvious as the length of the sound. Vowels can be classified according to whether the sound is short or held for a longer time:

Short	*Long*
pit	*peat*
pat	*part*
pot	*port*
pet	*pert*
putt	*poot*
put	

Activity 11.3 showed that the longer vowel sounds in the word 'maluma' are associated with a rounded shape, whereas the shorter sounds in 'takete' suggest an angular shape. Pupils could look again at the vowel sounds repeated in the poems by Wilfred Owen (Activity 11.5). There are many short vowel sounds in 'Dulce et Decorum Est', whereas more long vowels are used in 'Exposure'.

The vowels above are all monothongs – single sounds. Some vowel phonemes are diphthongs – slipping from one sound to another. Diphthongs may also convey a richer, rounded effect.

e + i	*as in*	*bay*
o + i		*boy*
a + i		*buy*
a + u		*bough*
er + u		*bow (i.e. ribbon in hair)*
i + er		*beer*
u + er		*sewer*
e + er		*hair*

Attitudes to regional accents

In Received Pronunciation (RP) – the standard – the two words 'put' and 'putt' have a different pronunciation. One feature of northern regional accents is the use of the same sound for both words. Attitudes to regional accents are often negative, leading some people to take elocution lessons to remove the traces of their accent. These attitudes are softening, as regional accents are given prominence in the media. But some stigma is still apparent: RP is used for national news reports, whereas northern accents are used to promote 'homely' products such as bread, tea and beer.

Rhythm

So far, we have looked at individual sounds and their effects. There are other aspects of spoken language that have an impact on meaning: volume, pitch, stress and intonation. These features are heard in the speaking voice, and can be conveyed in writing by visual signs. Punctuation marks, such as commas, full stops and semicolons, suggest pauses, whereas question marks and exclamation marks suggest a rising intonation. The use of different fonts and sizes of print can be used for emphasis, often suggesting the intonation of a speaking voice.

Line endings in poetry emphasise rhythmical breaks, sometimes in opposition to the sentence structure of prose. Poetry often uses a regular pattern of stresses – or metre. There are many books that deal with this feature of poetry, so it will not be included here. Instead, some examples are provided to show the rhythmical effects of certain grammatical structures.

Key words

repetition   parallelism   antithesis

Language in use

My name is Hinmatuheylocket. I have been asked to show you my heart. I am glad to have a chance to do so now. I want the white man to understand my people. He has many words to tell how my people look to him, but it does not require many words to speak the truth. What I have to say will come from my heart and I will speak it with a straight tongue. The Great Spirit is looking at me and will hear me. I have heard talk and talk, but nothing is done. Good words do not last long until they amount to something. Words do not pay for dead people. They do not pay for my country now overrun with white men. They do not protect my father's grave. They do not pay for my horses and cattle. Good words will not give me back my children. Good words will not give my people good health and stop them from dying. Good words will not get my people a home where they can live in peace and take care of themselves. I am tired of talk that comes to nothing. It makes my heart sick when I remember all the good words and all the broken promises.

(Chief Joseph, 1840–1904)

Repetition

Repetition – whether of individual words or structures – is always marked, in the sense that it is unusual. It is often a deliberate stylistic device for a particular effect. The example above is taken from an old recording of a Native American's speech to the US government. Even on the page, the rhythmical effects are moving.

Relatively simple sentence structures and vocabulary combine in a powerful expression of ideals and contradictions. There is marked repetition of 'words' and the related vocabulary, 'speak', 'hear', 'understand'. Chief Joseph contrasts the way words can be used: 'the truth', 'straight tongue', 'from the heart', as opposed to 'broken promises'. Ironically the phrase 'good words' is linked with the 'broken promises'. This is emphasised by the repetition of similar sentence structures, beginning with 'They do not . . .' Words are contrasted with actions, by the juxtaposition 'I have heard talk and talk, but nothing is done'.

The study of rhetoric provides technical terms for different types of repetition, but few of these terms are in common use today. The following examples from a website on rhetoric illustrate various types of repetition used by Shakespeare.

Parallelism: Similarity of structure in a pair or series of related words, phrases, or clauses

> And therefore, since I cannot prove a lover
> To entertain these fair well-spoken days,
> I am determinèd to prove a villain
> And hate the idle pleasures of these days.

> *(Richard III)*

Antithesis: Juxtaposition, or contrast of ideas or words in a balanced or parallel construction:

> Not that I loved Caesar less, but that I loved Rome more.

> *(Julius Caesar)*

The repetition of a word that ends one clause at the beginning of the next:

> My conscience hath a thousand several tongues,
> And every tongue brings in a several tale,
> And every tale condemns me for a villain.

> *(Richard III)*

Repetition of a word or phrase as the beginning of successive clauses:

> Mad world! Mad kings! Mad composition!

> *(King John)*

Two corresponding pairs arranged in a parallel inverse order:

> Fair is foul, and foul is fair

> *(Macbeth)*

Repetition broken up by one or more intervening words:

> Put out the light, and then put out the light.

> *(Othello)*

Repetition at the end of a clause of the word that occurred at the beginning of the clause:

> Blood hath bought blood, and blows have answer'd blows.
>
> *(King John)*

Frequent repetition of a phrase or question, dwelling on a point:

> Who is here so base that would be a bondman? If any, speak; for him I have offended.
> Who is here so rude that would not be a Roman? If any speak; for him have I offended.
>
> *(Julius Caesar)*

Repetition of a word or phrase at the end of successive clauses:

> I'll have my bond!
> Speak not against my bond!
> I have sworn an oath that I will have my bond.
>
> *(Merchant of Venice)*

Altering word order, or separation of words that belong together, for emphasis:

> Some rise by sin, and some by virtue fall.
>
> *(Measure for Measure)*

The repetition of conjunctions in a series of co-ordinate words, phrases, or clauses:

> If there be cords, or knives,
> Poison, or fire, or suffocating streams,
> I'll not endure it.
>
> *(Othello)*

Activity 11.7

- Identify the types of repetition used in the second part of the Native American speech, shown below.
- Comment on the effects.

> *If the white man wants to live in peace with the Indians he can live in peace. There need be no trouble. Treat all men alike. Give all the same law. Give the even chance to live and grow. All men were made by the same Great Spirit Chief. They are all brothers. The earth is the mother of all people and all people should have the same rights. If you tie a horse to a stake do you expect him to grow fat? If you pin an Indian to a small plot of earth, he will not be content, nor will he grow and prosper. I only ask of the government to be treated as all other men are treated. When I think of our condition, my heart is heavy. Let me be a free man: free to travel, free to stop; free to work, free to trade where I choose; free to choose my teachers, free to follow the religion of my fathers; free to think and talk and act for myself; and I will obey every law or submit to the penalty. There will be one sky above, one country around us, and one government for all. Then the Great Spirit Chief will smile upon this land. Hinmatuheylocket has spoken for his people.*
>
> *(Chief Joseph, 1840–1904)*

Balanced structures

The use of balanced structures is a feature of memorable sayings. Perhaps this type of structure suggests that the ideas are related, as strongly as in a mathematical formula.

The eyes of others are our prisons; their thoughts our cages.

(Virginia Woolf)

eyes	=	*prisons*
thoughts	=	*cages*

Every society honours its live conformists and its dead troublemakers.

(Mignon McLaughlin)

live	*vs*	*dead*
conformists	*vs*	*troublemakers*

yet:

dead troublemaker	=	*live conformist (both honoured by society)*

The use of a triple structure has always proved effective, its rhythm suggesting a build-up to a climax:

Men in great place are thrice servants: servants of the sovereign or state; servants of fame; and servants of business.

(Francis Bacon)

Often, this device is extended to a list of three or four items:

One equal temper of heroic hearts,
Made weak by time and fate, but strong in will
To strive, to seek, to find, and not to yield.

(Tennyson, 'Ulysses')

This chapter concludes with an activity that asks pupils to notice the combination of individual sounds with rhythmical grammatical structures.

Activity 11.8

- Note the repetition of grammatical structures, as well as sounds, in these extracts from political speeches.
- What effects do these types of repetition have?

> *Extract 1*
>
> *We shall not flag or fail. We shall go on to the end. We shall fight in France, we shall fight on the seas and oceans, we shall fight with growing confidence and growing strength in the air, we shall defend our island, whatever the cost may be, we shall fight on the beaches, we shall fight on the landing grounds, we shall fight in the fields and in the streets, we shall fight in the hills. We shall never surrender.*
>
> *(Winston Churchill, 'We Shall Fight them on the Beaches' speech, 1940)*

Extract 2

In 1931, ten years ago, Japan invaded Manchukuo – without warning. In 1935, Italy invaded Ethiopia – without warning. In 1938, Hitler occupied Austria – without warning. In 1939, Hitler invaded Czechoslovakia – without warning. Later in 1939, Hitler invaded Poland – without warning. And now Japan has attacked Malaya and Thailand – and the United States – without warning.

(Franklin D. Roosevelt, American declaration of war on Japan, 1941)

Extract 3

Thank you, Mr President, and thank you for your welcome. Thank you for your strength and for your leadership at this time. And I believe the alliance between the United States and Great Britain has never been in better or stronger shape.

Can I also offer the American people, on behalf of the British people, our condolences, our sympathy, our prayers for the lives of those who have fallen in this conflict, just as we have offered the condolence, the sympathy, and the prayers to the families of our own British servicemen?

(Tony Blair, joint press conference with President Bush at Camp David, 2003)

The next chapter moves on to the questions of meaning. It introduces some useful concepts from the study of semantics into the relationship between words and meanings.

12

Semantics

This chapter moves away from the structural features of language to explore the ways that words convey meanings. This area will be familiar to readers with a background in literature study. The key concept is 'figurative' language. Pupils quickly learn to use the terms in the Framework – metaphor, simile, connotation – to describe features of texts, but need to show a subtle understanding of the effects.

The study of semantics is an area where the disciplines of linguistics, literature, communication and cultural studies come together. It offers some useful concepts to develop pupils' awareness of the effects of vocabulary choice. The chapter begins with the most straightforward understanding of vocabulary – its 'literal' meaning. But a living language is rarely so straightforward.

> **Year 9:** recognise layers of meaning in the writer's choice of words, e.g. connotation, implied meaning, different types or multiple meanings

From a large vocabulary store, words can be chosen, not simply to communicate facts but to convey subtle shades of meaning, with underlying emotional effects or attitudes. The concept of emotive vocabulary is explored, introducing the terms 'collocation' and 'juxtaposition'. The ways that words occur in combination has an effect on their associated meanings.

> **Year 7:** recognise how writers' language choices can enhance meaning, e.g. repetition, emotive vocabulary

Activities encourage pupils to use dictionaries to explore the etymology of words to see how meanings may change over time. It is important for pupils to notice shifts in meaning from the literal to 'metaphorical'.

> **Year 8:** appreciate the impact of figurative language in texts

Poetry is often difficult – and rewarding – because of its use of fresh combinations of words, images and ideas. Examples of non-literary texts encourage pupils to become aware that metaphors are common, and significant, in everyday language.

The relationship between words and meaning

This opening section explores some ideas about the way words express meanings. On the one hand, there is the attitude that words are harmless – 'Sticks and stones may break my bones, but words can never harm me' – yet many people feel that it really does make a difference which words are used, that groups of people *can* be harmed by the words used to refer to them.

Key words
literal   denotation   synonym   antonym

Language in use

I pray thee, understand a plain man in his plain meaning.

(Shakespeare, The Merchant of Venice*)*

When I use a word... it means just what I choose it to mean – neither more nor less.

(Carroll, Through the Looking Glass*)*

The purpose of Newspeak was not only to provide a medium of expression for the world-view and mental habits proper to the devotees of IngSoc, but to make all other modes of thought impossible.

(Orwell, 1984*)*

That which we call a rose by any other name would smell as sweet.

(Shakespeare, Romeo and Juliet*)*

Does it matter what word we choose?

The quotations above introduce the discussion of words and meanings. The first suggests the 'common-sense' view that a word stands for something in the outside world. If this is the case, then words can be used to express a 'plain' meaning, with no ambiguity, or extra dimensions. But Lewis Carroll's character Humpty Dumpty (above) makes a claim that seems absurd – surely all language users must use words to mean the same thing, in order to communicate?

Can words *control* thought, so that it is impossible to have an idea for which no word exists? This is what Orwell's fictional language of Newspeak attempted to achieve – by ridding the language of words for undesirable concepts, the rulers hoped to eradicate such thoughts. The Sapir–Whorf hypothesis seems to support this view of words and meanings, suggesting that our perception of the world is affected – or even controlled – by the words we have to describe it. The example, often quoted but now considered misleading, is of the many words for 'snow' in the language of Eskimos. According to this argument, English language users cannot perceive subtly different types of 'snow', because we do not have the words in our vocabulary.

Does it make any difference what name is given to something? Would a rose 'smell as sweet' even if it was called a 'spludge' or 'wonkle'? As Chapter 11 on phonology, showed, naming can be significant. My alternative words certainly lack the pleasant sounds in the word 'rose', but perhaps other words would serve as well to name this flower. The movement, mocked by its opponents as 'political correctness', pointed out the negative effects of labelling people with disabilities as 'cripples', referring to people of African origin as 'coloured' and calling any females 'girls'.

Pupils should become aware of the power of words to do more than simply represent things in a neutral way. **Synonyms**, **antonyms** and the semantic concepts of **denotation**, connotation and collocation can be used to explore the complex relationships between words and meanings.

Denotation

The starting point in semantics is the concept of denotation. This term refers to the most straightforward relationship between a word and its meaning, i.e. a word stands for the object in the world that it represents. This relationship could be expressed by an equals sign, so that the word 'chair' = an object with four legs and a back. Dictionary definitions attempt to supply the denotative meanings of words, using synonyms or brief explanations:

> *chair, a separate seat for one person, usually having a back and four legs*

This is the **literal** meaning of the word 'chair'. But, even this simple word has acquired further meanings. It also means: a seat of authority; the person holding that position; to carry a person aloft in triumph. The concept of metaphorical extension of meaning is explored in a later section.

With concrete nouns, this relationship – a word denotes a specific aspect of the world – is reasonably convincing. But the meaning of abstract concepts is not so straightforward. Perhaps, like Humpty Dumpty, each person uses abstract words to mean 'just what I choose it to mean'. The following activity explores the meanings of the word 'love'.

Activity 12.1

- What does love mean?
- Does each person agree on the definition?
- How do you determine the meaning of this word?

The next section looks at ways that words acquire associated meanings.

Emotive language

Key words

emotive   connotation   collocation   juxtaposition   etymology

> ## Language in use
>
> *I am firm, you are stubborn, and he is pig-headed. (George Bernard Shaw)*
>
> | | | |
> |---|---|---|
> | *pro-choice* | *or* | *baby killers* |
> | *collateral damage* | *or* | *civilian casualties* |

Year 7: recognise how writers' language choices can enhance meaning, e.g. emotive vocabulary

The vocabulary of the English language has hundreds of thousands of words. As the above examples show, there are often various choices of words for a single concept. The first list of three ('firm', 'stubborn', 'pig-headed') could be extended further:

> *unyielding, determined, resolute, dogged, tenacious, obdurate, uncompromising, intransigent, mulish*

A thesaurus is a useful reference source for words related in meaning. The ability to vary the choice of vocabulary is an important skill, but pupils should be aware that these apparent synonyms do not simply convey a denotative meaning; words also acquire **emotive** meanings.

When talking about abortion, for example, the terms 'pro-choice' and 'baby killers' may denote the same thing, but from a very different viewpoint. Our vocabulary provides euphemisms to mask the harsh reality of taboo subjects, such as death, as in the vaguely detached reference to 'collateral damage'. Even the phrase 'civilian casualties' avoids the mention of death or connotations of outrage and blame, as might be found in a more emotive phrasing, such as 'the murder of innocent women and children'. The concept of connotation is a significant aspect of the meanings of words, particularly when grouping words as synonyms or antonyms.

Connotations

Although such groups of words can be termed synonyms, it is difficult to claim that they have the *same* meaning. As well as the literal, dictionary definition, each word has acquired slightly different associations, or emotive effects. The term **connotation** is used to distinguish the denotation of the word from its emotive meanings. There are many alternative words, for example, to denote mental illness:

> *mad, crazy, insane, deranged…*

Some terms are intended to convey a neutral description; others are derogatory. When the boxer, Frank Bruno, was admitted to hospital, the early editions of *The Sun* newspaper carried the headline 'Bonkers Bruno'. The public reaction was clearly far more sympathetic and later editions were quickly changed to 'Sad Bruno in Hospital'.

Etymology – word origins

Pupils should be aware that apparent synonyms carry emotive overtones. Such shades of meaning are acquired in their use over time, but can be explained partly by their **etymology**: their language origin. The main sources of English vocabulary are Anglo-Saxon, Latin and French. The vocabulary of Old English was Anglo-Saxon; the successive influences of Latin and French did not replace the original words, but added alternatives. In contemporary English, there are often at least three choices for a single concept:

Old English	French	Latin
kingly	royal	regal
killing	murder	homicide

However, these words are not simply interchangeable. They may simply occur in different contexts. The word 'kingly' is rarely used in modern English, so has an archaic flavour, for example,

> Thou who, in all Thy mighty, earthly marchings, ever cullest Thy selectest champions from the kingly commons; bear me out in it, O God!
>
> (Herman Melville, *Moby Dick*)

The word 'regal' tends to be used in brand names – Regal cinema/hotel, etc. or to describe a haughty manner. The word 'royal' has become the accepted term for describing the position of a monarchy.

The different words to refer to deliberate taking of a person's life are all in use today, but when one is substituted for another, different shades of meaning are conveyed. Ian Brady is described in the media as the 'Moors *murderer*'. He, however, describes his activities as 'periodic *homicide*', choosing a word derived from Latin, with more abstract, legal connotations. The Old English word 'killing' is perhaps too blunt to be mentioned.

The following activity focuses on another concept that has acquired a range of emotional attitudes. Body image has become such a sensitive issue in today's society, particularly for young females, that teachers may prefer to use this type of activity with less emotive words. 'Thin', or 'old', might be 'less contentious'.

Activity 12.2

- List as many synonyms as possible for the word 'fat'.
- Use a thesaurus to find further synonyms.
- Use a dictionary to check the etymology of each word.
- Use each of these words in a phrase.
- What does this suggest about the connotations of the word?

Collocation

The term **collocation** refers to 'the habitual co-occurrence of words' – in other words, their regular use in certain contexts. The fact that certain words often occur together affects their associated emotive meanings. For example, because the word chubby is often used to describe children, it has more positive overtones of health. The term 'obese' tends to be used in medical contexts, combined with terms such as 'diabetes' or 'heart disease', so has acquired more formal, negative connotations. The choice of one synonym rather than another is therefore not an arbitrary choice. The plain, denotative sense of the word includes various associated meanings, often connected with memories of previous uses, or collocations.

The following activity asks pupils to explore the collocations of the word 'swamp' and comment on the connotations that this word has acquired. These factors are just as significant as the literal dictionary definition.

Activity 12.3

What does the word 'swamp' mean? Check the dictionary definition.

- In what contexts do you recall the word being used?
- How does this affect its associated, emotive meanings?

Underlying attitudes and values

Year 9: recognise layers of meaning in the writer's choice of words, e.g. connotation, implied meaning, different types or multiple meanings

Pupils should be sensitive to the emotive associations of words. Politicians, for example, are often accused of 'spin'. This image suggests that their choice of words is not a straightforward representation, but a way of disguising some underlying attitudes. When the politician David Blunkett suggested that children of asylum seekers should be provided with separate education to avoid local schools being swamped, critics objected to his juxtaposition of the word 'swamped' with 'asylum seekers'. His response was that this reaction was 'oversensitive'. Perhaps, like Humpty Dumpty, he used this word to mean 'no more than a larger number than could be handled'; he wanted it to be understood in its 'plain' meaning. But the word 'swamp' has acquired further connotations. It regularly occurs in combination with asylum seekers, notably in hostile contexts and is used in media headlines:

Influx of asylum seekers threatening to swamp the UK

The image suggested by 'influx' relates the waters of a swamp to the powerful movement of the sea. This was used in a National Front newsletter a few years ago, when it referred to a 'flood tide of bogus asylum seekers'. This, in turn, may recall the image of 'rivers of blood' used in a famous speech of Enoch Powell in the late 1960s when he said:

like the Roman, I seem to see the River Tiber foaming with much blood

It is not only politicians who can imply underlying attitudes by their choice of vocabulary. In a radio programme about transsexuals, one speaker commented that, now that the laws have become more liberal, 'more are coming out of the woodwork'. His attitude was not overtly hostile, but his choice of words suggests an underlying fear. Words for pests and insects, such as cockroaches, are often found in collocation with the phrase 'out of the woodwork'.

The use of words with negative connotations is often a feature of persuasive language, where the speaker, or writer, wants to convey a feeling of threat. Tony Blair needed to justify his decision to declare war on Iraq, so, in a public speech, he used words such as 'systematically raped', 'pillaged', 'plundered a tiny nation', 'maimed and murdered', 'innocent children', 'war'. Other texts may present their point of view in more subtle ways.

The following activity asks pupils to use their understanding of grammar, as well as their awareness of vocabulary choice.

Activity 12.4

Identify the emotive language used in the following article.

- Which adjectives and adverbs could be deleted?
- What nouns (and noun phrases) are used to refer to the people mentioned?
- What noun phrases are used to refer to the drinks?
- What verbs are used to refer to drinking?
- How does the writer contrast 'today' with the past?
- What underlying attitudes are conveyed?

> I hate to say 'I told you so'. But those of us who spent the 1990s arguing that hysterical anti-drugs campaigns were targeting the wrong substances appear to have been proved right. The greatest threat to young people's health isn't Ecstasy, but the stuff that's freely available from the corner store to anyone wily enough to bribe their big brother into buying their booze.
>
> A third of 15- and 16-year-old girls binge-drink and the average 15-year-old consumes 11.3 units of alcohol a week. Even without the shocking statistics, it's plain there's a serious problem. Groups of sozzled adolescents staggering along the high street are a common sight, and from what I hear few party guests over the age of 13 expect to be offered anything softer than alcopops.
>
> Underage drinking isn't new, of course, and most mums and dads probably downed a few ciders during their own teens. But at the risk of sounding like an old crone, the youth of today are drinking in increasingly dangerous quantities, with alarming frequency. And for the first time, young women are drinking more than their male counterparts. Significantly more girls than boys now binge.

Juxtaposition

The literary term **juxtaposition** is similar to the concept of collocation, but it refers to particular instances of unusual combinations. This creative use of vocabulary is often a feature of poetry. The phrase 'a grief ago' (Dylan Thomas) uses the abstract noun 'grief' in the usual place of words for time: 'minute', 'year', etc. The reader must work out a connection in order to understand this new idea. The juxtaposition emphasises the incalculable length of time that grief lasts.

Activity 12.5

- Note the unusual juxtaposition of vocabulary in this poem.
- How do you interpret the meanings suggested?
- What other language features are significant?

Siege

he peeps	i duck
i shoot	he ducks
i wave	he waves back
i peep	he shoots
he waves	i shoot
and duck	i peep
i peep again	
he's dead	
	draped across his turret
he smiles	my arrow tickles
the inside of his head	

(Johnny Byrne)

Figurative language

Key words

figurative language   images, imagery   metaphor   simile
metonym   symbol

This article explodes a common myth that figurative language – metaphors, in particular – is only used in literary texts. Pupils should be aware of this use of language in all texts.

Year 8: appreciate the impact of figurative language in texts

As Goddard observes, metaphors in everyday language tend to pass unnoticed. Perhaps these metaphors from the extract were 'invisible': 'tall stories'; 'looking at' metaphor; talk as 'a zone'; talk as 'money'; and metaphors as 'people'.

The Framework for Key Stages 3 and 4 uses the following terms to refer to non-literal uses of vocabulary. The phrase **figurative language** is the overall term for the extension of meaning from the literal to the metaphorical. This 'umbrella' term includes various devices for conveying non-literal meanings: simile, symbol, metonym, metaphor. The first two are so familiar that a brief comment is provided. Although the term 'metonym' is not explicitly required, Activity 12.6 demonstrates that pupils are aware of this device for conveying implied meanings. Metaphors are explored in detail later.

The term **simile** is used for explicit comparisons, when the words 'like' or 'as' are used:

> My love is like a red, red rose. (Robert Burns)
> I felt as sick as a parrot.

These are simple to identify, but pupils should notice whether the simile is effective. Some have become clichés; others may be unconvincing or strange.

> The pleasure hit me like a runaway baboon. (Häagen Däaz ice cream advertisement)
> Eyebrows like caterpillars on the tree of knowledge (Saul Bellow)

The term **symbol** is used for a sign which stands for something in a particular social community. Colours, for example, acquire symbolic meanings: black for death, red for danger or passion, white for purity, etc. These symbolic meanings may vary from culture to culture, or over time.

The term **metonym** is used when an attribute is used to represent the whole, as in:

The keel [ship] ploughed the waves [sea].
The crown [title of king] passed to Prince Harry.

Pupils should notice the way certain physical aspects are used to represent general characteristics. Such meanings are often specific to a particular social context. In contemporary language, these attributes are used to suggest a particular type of person or lifestyle:

a white van man
Essex girls
bling

Year 8: experiment with figurative language in conveying a sense of character and setting

The following creative writing activity uses pupils' implicit awareness of metonyms.

Activity 12.6

Imagine a country pub. A man walks in. He is wearing a grey suit, a gold watch and two large rings on one hand. He has a scar on his cheek. There is a woman with him.

- Write a description of the woman's appearance in five sentences.
- Listen to others' description of the woman.
- Comment on any interesting similarities and differences.
- What 'story' is suggested about these two people?

Dead metaphors

A **metaphor**, like these other figurative uses of words, suggests a connection, usually between a physical entity and an abstract idea. Unusual metaphors draw attention to themselves, but many have become so familiar that they may pass unnoticed.

Many common words in the language began as metaphors, but the literal meaning has been forgotten. A person described as 'keen' on sport, or having a 'keen' interest in science, is understood to be enthusiastic; the original meaning of 'sharp', as in 'keen weapons' is no longer used. The term 'dead metaphor' is used for such examples. Any fairly large dictionary provides details of the word's derivation in square brackets at the end. For example, the word 'muscle' derives from the Latin word *musculus*, meaning 'mouse'.

Activities such as the following provide practice in using dictionaries, as well as revealing some interesting aspects of language change.

Activity 12.7

- Use a good dictionary to look up the derivation of these words.
- What connection can you see between the original and the contemporary meaning of the word?

    monster, insult, person, manufacture, anarchy, horrid, hysterical, cynic

Images

The term **imagery** is often used as an alternative for 'figurative language', as abstract ideas are often conveyed by visual **images**. Imagery may also use the other physical senses of hearing, touch, taste and smell. These categories are used in the following activity, as a way of collecting examples of figurative language in common use.

Activity 12.8

- Group these metaphors according to the sense to which they appeal: sight, hearing, touch, taste, smell.
    - *a brilliant idea*
    - *Chill out.*
    - *The sweet smell of success*
    - *Things are going smoothly.*
    - *My memory is a bit cloudy.*
    - *boiling mad*
    - *That voices grates on me.*
    - *a sour note*
    - *This is hard to do.*
    - *She thundered out of the room.*
    - *a tepid reception*
    - *I can't see the point.*
    - *something to chew on*
    - *the high note of the evening*
    - *a deep, dark secret*
- Add other expressions that appeal to the five senses.

Spatial images

Spatial concepts are often used in figurative senses. We talk of getting ahead or falling behind; feeling high or low; including people or leaving them out. Pupils might collect common expressions connected to these physical positions:

> *up vs down*
> *in front vs behind*
> *inside vs outside*

Implied attitudes

These spatial metaphors are probably shared by all cultures – it is unlikely that the figurative sense of 'down' or 'outside' could have positive associations. However, some metaphorical uses of language may reflect the attitudes and values of a particular social group. A Saudi Arabian student commented on the strange amount of freedom women were permitted in our culture, saying, 'My wife is like gold. I keep her in a box.' This metaphor may seem repressive, but there are related metaphors of possession in contemporary discourse about male/female relationships: 'bonds', 'ties', 'to have and to hold', etc.

The following activities explore the figurative language used to convey ideas above love and relationships.

Activity 12.9

- What ideas are expressed about love and relationships in the following examples?
- Collect other examples of expressions about love and relationships, e.g. from the lyrics of popular songs.

> *This relationship isn't going anywhere.*
> *They're in a dead-end relationship.*
> *I was taken for a ride.*
>
> *We were made for each other.*
> *She is my other/better half.*
> *He is a perfect match.*
>
> *My friend stole my boyfriend.*
> *I'm going to get him back.*
> *Why not take all of me?*
>
> *The magic is gone.*
> *She charmed him.*
> *I was entranced.*
>
> *I'm crazy about him.*
> *I'm just wild about Harry.*
> *She is madly in love.*
>
> *(further examples can be found on linguist, Robin Lakoff's website)*

Application to language change

Colloquial expressions about love and relationships may change over time. The image of 'being left on the shelf' seems rather old-fashioned in its negative attitude to a life outside a relationship, but the more modern expression 'dumped' is even more despairing. Problem pages are a source of contemporary figurative language about love and relationships.

Activity 12.10

- Identify the metaphors used in the following problem-page letter and response.
- What do these suggest about contemporary attitudes to love and relationships?

> #### My guy's leaving me
>
> I've been dating an older boy for about a year (I'm 16 and he's 18). The age difference has meant nothing to us – until now. You see, he's off to university this autumn, which means we'll have to split up. I reckon we could still carry on seeing each other, but he says it's best to end it, rather than letting things drag on any longer. Is this just his way of dumping me?
>
> Carol, Liverpool
>
> #### Response
>
> For many, going to university is a major step 'cause it's symbolic of gaining independence. Of course, some find it hard, so they keep relationships at home going to give them something to run back to. But your boyfriend is trying to sever these links before he goes. It's a brave move on his part, and an honest one. He could let things tick over and just fizzle out, but instead he's making a clean break now. It's hard, but I think you should accept his decision. If you kept it going, you may be let down less kindly later on. I know it hurts, but breaking up now will be less painful than being unsure about what he's up to when he's away. My advice is to let him go.

Application to literary texts

There are so many ready-made phrases to describe emotions that it is hard to find a way to make such clichés 'come to life'. In literary texts, a familiar metaphor is often developed in unusual ways, as the following activity shows.

Activity 12.11

Match the everyday metaphors to ideas expressed in the following literary texts.

Familiar metaphors

- We were made for each other.
- My legs turned to jelly.

- Fear gripped me.
- the tears of a clown
- putting a brave face on it
- Love is blind.
- You hurt me.
- I've been left out in the cold.
- I'm out of my mind.

Literary texts

See also *'Not Waving but Drowning'* by Stevie Smith.

Extract 1

You fit into me
Like a hook in an eye
A fish hook
An open eye.

(Margaret Atwood)

Extract 2

Symptoms of Love
Love is a universal migraine
A bright stain on the vision
Blotting out reason.

(Robert Graves)

Extract 3

Monkey Nuts
Her arm was around his waist, she drew him closely to her with a soft pressure that made his bones rotten.

(D. H. Lawrence)

Extract 4

Anita and Me
I was hot and I could feel beads of sweat and fear threading themselves into a necklace of guilt, just where my itchy flesh met the collar of my starched cotton dress.

(Meera Syal)

Integrating grammar and semantics

This area of semantics plays to the strengths of teachers with a literary background. Although the Framework may seem to emphasise unfamiliar grammatical terminology, pupils' understanding of ways meanings are conveyed remains central to language study.

The final activity combines awareness of grammar and figurative language in analysis of a literary text.

Activity 12.12

This extract is taken from Charles Dickens' novel *Hard Times*. Mr Gradgrind is visiting a classroom.

- What qualities does the writer convey about each character by his use of images?
- What does this use of imagery suggest about the role of each character in the novel (hero/heroine, villain/victim, etc.)?
- How does the grammar reflect the choice of vocabulary?

> *Thomas Gradgrind, sir. A man of realities. A man of fact and calculations. A man who proceeds upon the principle that two and two are four, and nothing over, and who is not to be talked into allowing for anything over. Thomas Gradgrind, sir – peremptorily Thomas — Thomas Gradgrind. With a rule and a pair of scales, and the multiplication table always in his pocket, sir, ready to weigh and measure any parcel of human nature, and tell you exactly what it comes to. It is a mere question of figures, a case of simple arithmetic. You might hope to get some other nonsensical belief into the head of George Gradgrind, or Augustus Gradgrind or John Gradgrind, or Joseph Gradgrind (all suppositions, no existent persons), but into the head of Thomas Gradgrind – no, sir!*
>
> *In such terms Mr. Gradgrind always mentally introduced himself, whether to his private circle of acquaintance, or to the public in general. In such terms, no doubt, substituting the words 'boys and girls', for 'sir', Thomas Gradgrind now presented Thomas Gradgrind to the little pitchers before him, who were to be filled so full of facts.*
>
> *Indeed, as he eagerly sparkled at them from the cellarage before mentioned, he seemed a kind of cannon loaded to the muzzle with facts, and prepared to blow them clean out of the regions of childhood at one discharge. He seemed a galvanizing apparatus, too, charged with a grim mechanical substitute for the tender young imaginations that were to be stormed away.*
>
> *The square finger, moving here and there, lighted suddenly on Bitzer, perhaps because he chanced to sit in the same ray of sunlight which, darting in at one of the bare windows of the intensely white-washed room, irradiated Sissy. For, the boys and girls sat on the face of the inclined plane in two compact bodies, divided up the centre by a narrow interval; and Sissy, being at the corner of a row on the sunny side, came in for the beginning of a sunbeam, of which Bitzer, being at the corner of a row on the other side, a few rows in advance, caught the end. But, whereas the girl was so dark-eyed and dark-haired, that she seemed to receive a deeper and more lustrous colour from the sun, when it shone upon her, the boy was so light-eyed and light-haired that the self-same rays appeared to draw out of him what little colour he ever possessed. His cold eyes would hardly have been eyes, but for the short ends of lashes*

which, by bringing them into immediate contrast with something paler than themselves, expressed their form. His short-cropped hair might have been a mere continuation of the sandy freckles on his forehead and face. His skin was so unwholesomely deficient in the natural tinge, that he looked as though, if he were cut, he would bleed white.

She curtseyed again, and would have blushed deeper, if she could have blushed deeper than she had blushed all this time. Bitzer, after rapidly blinking at Thomas Gradgrind with both eyes at once, and so catching the light upon his quivering ends of lashes that they looked like the antennae of busy insects, put his knuckles to his freckled forehead, and sat down again.

The next chapters look at the area of discourse studies, introducing terms and concepts for the study of whole texts in their social context.

Discourse

The final chapters move on to the study of whole texts. The progression of chapters in the book mirrors the organisation of the Framework of Teaching English into the three levels of Word, Sentence and Text.

TABLE 13.1 Chapter topics

	Word	Sentence	Text
Chapters 2 and 3	morphology		
Chapters 4–10		syntax	
Chapter 11	phonology		
Chapter 12	semantics		
Chapter 13			discourse
Chapter 14			pragmatics

This chapter introduces some useful, accessible concepts from the study of 'discourse'. This term signals a shift in interest – from words and sentences in isolation to the way language works in its full context. This may come as a relief to those sceptical about the value of a 'microscopic' analysis of language. Many aspects of discourse studies are familiar to teachers with a background in literature study. The recommendations in the Framework refer to key concepts from discourse, sometimes using alternative terms. For example,

Genre	*Forms*	*Text types*
context	*situation*	*circumstances*
register	*formality*	

Year 8: develop different ways of linking paragraphs, using a range of strategies to improve cohesion and coherence, e.g. choice of connectives, reference back, linking phrases

The first section explores the structure of written texts – the ways links between paragraphs are signposted.

Year 9: review ability to write for a range of purposes and audiences

Year 8: explore and use different degrees of formality in written and oral texts, e.g. formal speeches, informal journals

Year 7: revise the conventions of explanation, which maintains the use of the present tense and impersonal voice

Year 8: recognise the conventions of some common literary forms … and explore how a particular text adheres to or deviates from established conventions

The key concepts of genre, purpose and audience are used to develop pupils' awareness of context.

The concept of register is used to explore the ways that language varies according to the context.

Some activities explore the conventions associated with different genres and the effects of innovation.

Text structure

Key words
cohesion: lexical cohesion, grammatical cohesion pronouns   connectives   reference back linking phrases

Language in use
losing the thread *tying up loose ends* *cotton on* *spin a yarn*

The phrases above show the recurrent metaphor of woven cloth as an image for language use. Although individual sentences may be well constructed, they need to be connected to each other in ways that aid comprehension of the overall argument. They need to cohere, or stick together.

In everyday use, the words 'discourse' and 'text' are used to mean, respectively, 'talking' and 'writing'. Yet the two concepts are closely related. The Latin root of the term 'discourse' comes from the word *discursus*, meaning 'to run'; the Latin root of the term 'text' comes from *texere*, meaning 'to weave'. Speakers and writers may 'run on and on', but effective speech and writing requires clear patterning, rather like material is constructed from loose threads.

Cohesion

Year 8: develop different ways of linking paragraphs, using a range of strategies to improve cohesion and coherence, e.g. choice of connectives, referencing back, linking phrases

There are two types of **cohesion**: **lexical** and **grammatical**. In the former, the use of related vocabulary items form the threads that weave a text into a coherent whole. In the latter, use of **pronouns** and **connectives** indicate the links between sentences.

Lexical cohesion

direct repetition	*e.g. the word <u>creature</u>*
synonyms	*e.g. <u>creature</u>/<u>animal</u>/<u>being</u>*
antonyms	*e.g. <u>animate</u> vs <u>non-animate</u>*
super-ordination	*e.g. <u>creature</u> – <u>reptile</u> – <u>snake</u> – <u>python</u>*
specific-general reference	*e.g. <u>snake</u> – <u>poisonous snake</u>, <u>pet snake</u>*

NB The technical term 'super-ordination' refers to a hierarchy of terms, so that a general term such as 'food' includes many subcategories, including 'pasta', which can be further specified into types, such as 'macaroni'. Specific types of macaroni can be named: 'quick cook', 'wholewheat', etc. This relationship is termed 'specific–general reference'.

Grammatical cohesion

There are four types of grammatical cohesion: pronoun reference, connectives, **linking phrases** and **reference back**:

pronoun reference	*e.g. <u>snakes</u>: <u>it</u>, <u>they</u>*
connectives	*e.g. <u>for example</u>, <u>on the other hand</u>*
linking phrases	*e.g. <u>in the desert</u>, <u>in many cases</u>*
reference back	*e.g. <u>such snakes</u>, <u>these snakes</u>*

The following activity provides practice in identifying the cohesive devices used within a paragraph.

> **Year 8:** identify the overall structure of a text to identify how key ideas are developed, e.g. through the organisation of the content and the patterns of language used

Activity 13.1

- Identify the types of lexical cohesion (underlined) in the following text.
- Identify the grammatical cohesion – including linking phrases indicating chronology (sequence of time).

> **Victor, the Wild Child of Aveyron**
>
> <u>Victor</u>, a <u>boy</u> of about 11 or 12, was discovered foraging for roots and acorns in the woods near Aveyron, France in 1799. <u>Victor</u> was taken to Paris, where he <u>appeared</u> to be <u>human</u> only in appearance. <u>Victor</u> <u>behaved</u> like an <u>animal</u>, ate rotten food with pleasure, was incapable of distinguishing <u>hot</u> from <u>cold</u>, and spent much of his time rocking back and forth like a <u>caged animal</u>. <u>Victor</u> was taken into the care of the brilliant scientist, Dr Jean-Marc-Gaspard Itard, who dedicated himself to the <u>education</u> of the <u>lad</u>. <u>Victor</u> proved to be a very difficult subject. Over the years, <u>Victor</u> only <u>learned</u> two terms, 'lait', and 'oh Dieu'. His <u>sense</u> of <u>touch</u> seemed to be far more important than his <u>sense</u> of <u>sight</u>, he did not demonstrate an ability to distinguish <u>right</u> from <u>wrong</u>, and like Peter before him, he was indifferent to sex. He did however, <u>learn</u> some <u>menial tasks</u>, such as <u>setting a table</u>. <u>Victor</u> <u>lived</u> the rest of his life in the care of his housekeeper, and died in 1828 at the age of 40.
>
> (http://www.bbc.co.uk/dna/h2g2/alabaster/A269840)

Discourse markers

Year 8: develop different ways of linking paragraphs, using a range of strategies to improve cohesion and coherence, e.g. choice of connectives, reference back, linking phrases

Year 7: organise texts in ways appropriate to their content, e.g. by chronology, priority, comparison, and signpost this clearly to the reader

Year 7: identify the main points, processes and ideas in a text and how they are sequenced and developed by the writer

Year 7: tailor the structure, vocabulary and delivery of a talk or presentation so that listeners can follow it

Year 7: recognise the way familiar spoken texts, e.g. directions, explanations, are organised, and identify their typical features, e.g. of vocabulary or tone

The single paragraph above used various devices to make it cohesive. Pupils also need to recognise and use a range of connectives between paragraphs.

NB Such devices are also termed 'discourse markers' or 'transition devices'. There is useful material on transition devices on various websites. (www.sdc.uwo.ca/writing/handouts).

Key connectives (discourse markers) are grouped in the Framework by their function. For example,

addition	*also, furthermore, moreover*
opposition	*however, nevertheless, on the other hand*

Activities based on jumbled paragraphs can make pupils aware of the way texts are organised. The individual paragraphs of a text can be cut up and rearranged. If the text is cohesive, it should be possible to work out the original sequence of paragraphs. Pupils may be asked to add connectives to signpost the links between paragraphs.

Written texts can use visual markers, other than paragraph breaks, to signpost their structure. Talks and other spoken presentations need to use aural clues, such as pauses, stress and intonation, to highlight the verbal markers of structure.

Activity 13.2

The following extracts were written by pupils in Year 12.

- What visual signposts are used to make the structure of the written text clear?
- What verbal clues indicate the sequence of points in the script for a talk?
- How might the speaker use tone of voice to highlight this structure?

Extract 1

ADVICE FOR TEACHERS FACED WITH THE PROBLEM OF BULLYING

This leaflet is aimed to help you be more aware of bullying in schools. It is not an easy issue to assess as it is fairly complex. There are however main standards to be met to help ensure that this problem is minimised. The school needs to be run efficiently and effectively in order for students to feel at ease with the environment.

WHAT TEACHERS MUST DO TO HELP

1 Ensure that discipline is kept high at all times.

2 Do not let the pupils run the lesson. You are in control. It is important to realise that they cannot manipulate the teacher. You have the power, it is there for the taking.

3 Bullying falls into many categories. There are emotional and physical attributes and children are considerably clever at hiding these.

The teacher has to be exceptionally aware of how individuals act. It is important to realise that the child will not open up to the teacher because they are afraid. Perhaps it would be important to try and get to know the individuals but making sure you keep a dividing line between pupils and teachers. This may help to see the individual's behaviour. How someone acts will change when situations alter, in this case bullying.

HOW EASY IS IT TO PICK UP?

No one is telepathic! As long as teachers have constant communication with students, then it is possible that children who are upset will have the incentive to come and speak out.

Extract 2

SCRIPTS FOR TALK

Hi folks, it's Abbie Smithers here and I'm not going to harp on about courses, exams, revision and study, although those are all very important to your time here at [name of school]. I am here to talk about the fun things that happen, the sports events, the fancy dress for charity, the social events, dances, bands, parties, the whole lot. As those of you doing sports courses already know we have a fully equipped gym and swimming pool, which anyone can use for a minimal cost. How about that for getting fit! Still keeping to the sports side of things, we run many clubs from table tennis to swimming to athletics. These are available to all. How about social events? Wow! We have lots. You can come to anything from a drama group performance, an end of year dance, check our sports teams, or watch a battle of the bands.

In these examples, the pupils have used clear devices for signposting the progression of ideas. The vocabulary and sentence structures also convey the degree of formality (register) they felt appropriate for the situation. The next section provides a framework for exploring this aspect of language variation.

Register – degrees of formality

Key words
register   formality   situation   context   genre

Language in use

No smoking.
Stub it out!
Smoking is not permitted.
Please refrain from smoking.
Your co-operation in refraining from smoking is appreciated.
Patrons are respectfully reminded that smoking is not allowed on these premises.

Year 8: recognise how the degree of formality influences word choice

The term **register** is borrowed from the field of music and refers to the varying degrees of formality that may be conveyed in language. As the examples above show, the 'no smoking' message can be expressed in various ways, depending on the situation. Choice of vocabulary and sentence structures affects the degree of **formality** of the message.

Activity 13.3

- Identify the range of colloquial and formal vocabulary in the 'no smoking' notices above.
- What do you notice about the variety of structures? For example,
    - brief vs complex sentences
    - direct imperatives vs passive voice

Situation of language use

A brief definition of register is 'The way language varies according to situation'.

The alternative term 'formality' is often used, but pupils should be aware that this does not refer to a simple distinction between two styles of language: formal vs informal. The notion of *degrees* of formality is important, so that language use can be seen as a subtle continuum, ranging from the most formal, impersonal style through to the most personal, informal style of communication between close friends. It is obvious that one significant aspect of language use is the people involved and their relationship. This may be the writer and reader(s); the speaker and their audience; or the participants in a two-way conversation. But there are other aspects of the situation that influence the register. The following framework (Holmes, 1992) suggests that the **situation** includes these four social factors and dimensions:

Factor	Dimension
participants	*social distance*
	social status
purpose	*function*
topic	
setting	*formality*

This is similar to the concepts used in the classroom, sometimes abbreviated to acronyms such as GAP or SPAG, which refer to the familiar terms:

Subject	*topic*
Purpose	
Audience	*participants*
Genre	

This framework includes the extra factor of the **genre** of language used. The two main divisions between the modes of *spoken* and *written* language use can each be divided into more specific types, or forms, of language use: a spoken conversation or scripted speech; a written letter, notice, leaflet, report, review, narrative, poem, etc. This shorthand version of the **context** – or situation – is useful as an *aide-mémoire* for pupils, but needs to be used with some subtlety. It is not enough to 'pigeonhole' a text with four simple labels, as the next activity shows.

Activity 13.4

- Identify the subject, purpose, audience and genre of the following text.
- What register (degree of formality) is used?
- After reading the commentary, use the amended framework to develop the analysis of register.

> *Mike. Excuse my shabby handwriting. I was walking into my room this morning 2 find a world war 3 battleground. I trust you (to a certain extent), and I thought u would clear up. evidently this is not what u had on your Mind Brain empteyhole thoughts. So I am giving u a second chance. I'm @ Jacks and if it is not clean then heads will roll and I shall kick you 'James and the giant Peaches'. k?*
>
> *(note left by a 13-year-old boy to his 12-year-old brother; originally handwritten, with words 'Mind Brain empteyhole' crossed out, but legible)*

Extending analysis of register

This analysis overlooks the complexity of the register, which actually shifts between informal and more formal, in order to achieve the desired effect. (See Activity 13.7 on page 199.)

Pupils should think of the purposes (note the plural) of language use, and develop the concept of audience to include the relationship, or interaction, between writer and reader. The following framework of concepts (Hudson, 1980) may be useful, each represented as a continuum:

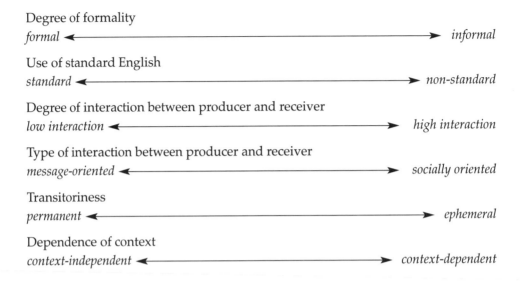

Degree of formality
formal ←————————————————————————————————→ *informal*

Use of standard English
standard ←————————————————————————————————→ *non-standard*

Degree of interaction between producer and receiver
low interaction ←————————————————————————————→ *high interaction*

Type of interaction between producer and receiver
message-oriented ←————————————————————————→ *socially oriented*

Transitoriness
permanent ←————————————————————————————————→ *ephemeral*

Dependence of context
context-independent ←————————————————————————→ *context-dependent*

Application to writing skills

Year 8: explore and use different degrees of formality in written and oral texts, e.g. formal speeches, informal journals

Pupils can transfer this awareness of the register of texts to their own language use. Activity 13.5 asks pupils to draft a written notice for a particular situation. They should then choose the most effective and explain their reasons.

Activity 13.5

Your school wants to prevent people from consuming food or drink in classrooms.

- Draft a notice for the classroom wall.
- Work in groups to select the most effective.
- Explain your reasons for this choice, using terms such as purpose and audience.

Degrees of formality in language

It is helpful to isolate one or two factors of language in use, in order to focus on subtle differences. Teachers could collect a group of texts, all of a similar genre but with significant differences of purpose and audience. If the texts are produced on individual cards, pupils can work in groups, ranking them in a scale of formality and discussing possible alternatives. This intuitive awareness can be developed by explaining the significant factors of each situation. The identification of purpose and audience should be extended, using some of the concepts suggested above.

Pupils should then identify some features of language use that convey the appropriate degree of formality. The following language features are often markers of the degree of formality:

Formal	*Informal*
	Word choice
standard English	*non-standard, colloquial, slang, abbreviations*
polysyllabic words	*monosyllabic words*
Latinate vocabulary	*vocabulary of Anglo-Saxon origin*
	Syntax
complex structures	*non-standard and simple structures*
impersonal address	*direct address with first and second person pronouns*
passive voice	*interrogatives and imperative structures*

The above note could be included with the texts in the following activity, to explore differences in the style and situation of letters.

Activity 13.6

- Rank the following short letters according to degree of formality.
- Explain the differences in situation/context of each.
- Identify features of vocabulary or syntax that convey the degree of formality in the third extract.

Extract 1

Is this your cat?

A ginger male cat has been frequenting the student house on St George's Rd due to a recent incident, the cat will have to be taken to a cat rescue centre if the owner cannot be contacted. If you are the owner of this cat or know the person who is, could you please contact me (Louise) on: 0945 532 7904 (5–8pm)

Thanks

(a typed notice posted through letterboxes in a local area)

Extract 2

A perplexed six-year-old in my school recently wanted to know what 'oles' were after hearing a presenter on a Schools Television Broadcast talk about 'oles and fings' ('holes and things').

We no longer use the programme in question, but I do wonder whether it is me or the programme producers who are at fault. Should I accept declining standards of speech or should the producers accept some responsibility for setting higher standards, by giving better examples of correct pronunciation and join me in striving to pass on the beauty of our Mother Tongue?

Patricia Seekings
Acremont School, Ely
(letter published in the Daily Express)

Extract 3

SOMESUCH COLLEGE OF TECHNOLOGY AND ARTS

SAFETY NOTICE CONCERNING COLLEGE LIFTS

Staff should be aware that there appears to be another outbreak of certain students misbehaving in lifts in a way which puts themselves and other students at risk. This clearly is unacceptable and I should be grateful for your co-operation in taking preventative action when this occurs.

I have also asked that all students be reminded that vandalism in lifts could lead to disciplinary action. One lift is already out of commission as a direct result of vandalism. If this continues the lifts may have to be withdrawn from use. The maximum capacity for lifts is 23 and under no circumstances should this be exceeded.

I would also remind staff and students that we all have a duty under Health and Safety legislation to ensure safety practices within the work environment.

A. N. OTHER
PRINCIPAL

(memo displayed in FE college)

Implied meanings

Year 7: identify the ways implied and explicit meanings are conveyed

An awareness of register can help pupils identify implied meanings in texts. A high degree of formality often conveys a position of authority for the writer and a corresponding lack of status for the audience. An informal style often suggests an equal relationship between writer and audience.

Pupils need to be aware of these implications of the degree of formality they adopt. The flyer addressed to neighbours in Activity 13.6 manages to combine politeness with friendliness. In some situations, the reader may feel patronised if the tone seems inappropriate. The advice leaflet on bullying (Activity 13.2. Extract 1) uses a formal style to address teachers, suggesting a position of authority, although the writer is a pupil.

There is a trend towards increasing informality in many contexts of contemporary language use. Perhaps this reflects more democratic, equal relationships in today's society. People are often addressed by first name – often to the dismay of older people – and the use of colloquial vocabulary, or even slang, is common in broadsheet newspapers, political speeches and academic texts. Pupils should be aware of this, but it is safer to err on the side of caution in public forms of language, where the audience is outside their familiar sphere, or where the purpose is serious. It is not appropriate, for example, to refer to authors by their first name alone in essays: it may be 'Jane Austen', or 'Austen', but never 'Jane'.

Purpose and audience

In the secondary English curriculum, pupils need to practise writing for a range of different purposes and audiences:

- to inform, explain, describe
- to persuade, argue, advise
- to analyse, review, comment
- to imagine, explore, entertain.

Year 7: present texts with readers and purpose in mind

The Framework lists the purposes required in four groups. This neat outline may suggest that it is straightforward to distinguish the purpose of any piece of writing and the style needed. But writing to entertain takes many forms. By its nature, imaginative writing is innovative, so exposure to a range of literary, non-fiction texts provides pupils with ideas for their own writing.

Some overtly persuasive texts do have the features listed (in the *standards.dfes* website): *emphasises key points and articulates logical links in the argument.* However, many writers convey their point of view with a mixture of information and entertainment.

Perhaps it is easier to identify the main stylistic conventions of informative and instructional texts (also *standards.dfes*):

> **information**, which maintains the use of the present tense and the third person, organises and links information clearly; incorporates examples
> **instructions**, which are helpfully sequenced and signposted, deploy imperative verbs and provide clear guidance

Examples of texts written for these purposes can be used as models for pupils' own writing. Their understanding of grammatical terms and concepts can be applied in reading the text and then in redrafting their own work.

The following activity uses informative texts with slightly different audiences. One is from an encyclopedia of science aimed at junior school children, while the other is from an encyclopedia of history with a more general audience.

Activity 13.7

- Identify the topic, purpose and audience of these two texts.
- Note the types of sentence structure and vocabulary used in each.

Extract 1

Volcanoes

Most volcanoes are found near the coast or under the ocean. They usually form at plate edges. Here crust movement allows hot molten rock called magma to rise up from inside the Earth and burst through the crust. Hot magma is called lava when it flows out of a volcano. Ash, steam and gas also spew out and cause great destruction.

Extinct volcano

Castle Rock, Edinburgh is an extinct volcano. It has not erupted for 340 million years. An extinct volcano such as this is not expected to erupt again.

Dormant volcano

If scientists believe a volcano may erupt again, perhaps because it gives off volcanic gases, it is called dormant. Mt Rainier, USA is described as dormant.

(*Dorling Kindersley* Visual Encyclopedia of Science)

Extract 2

Jarrow March

The plight of the unemployed in Britain during the Great Depression was forcefully underlined by the Jarrow March of October 1936. By 1935, unemployment in Jarrow in northeast England, an area almost entirely dependent on shipbuilding, had reached 73 percent. Prompted by the National Unemployed Workers Movement, 200 Jarrow shipworkers walked the 300 miles (483 km) to London to petition Parliament. It was a movingly vivid demonstration of the desperation to which they, and millions of others, had been reduced.

(*Dorling Kindersley* Timelines World of History)

Genre

In the study of discourse, **genre** is defined as 'the stylistic characteristics associated with a particular form of language'. Pupils need to become aware of the conventions of a variety of genres outside their immediate social experience, in order that they do not use inappropriate forms – often those of informal conversations, emails or text messaging.

Language in use

Good morning everybody... I want to see how QUIETLY you can all leave.

All rise... The session is now adjourned.

Dear Occupier... Apply now if you wish to claim your place in the prize draw.

It was a dark and stormy night and the brigands were there... The villagers could now live in peace.

The way a text opens and closes often provides a clear indication of its genre. Teachers could provide pupils with the first and last sentence of a variety of texts and ask them to identify the genre. The examples above follow the expected conventions of (in order):

- spoken: a junior school assembly
- spoken: court proceedings
- written: junk mail promotion
- written or spoken: narrative.

Innovation in language use

An awareness of genre is an important part of a reader's competence – any text is interpreted within a framework of our expectations of language use. Of course, the conventions are not absolutely fixed, so pupils should also notice deviations from the expected norm, or any crossover between genres.

> **Year 8:** recognise the conventions of some common forms and explore how a particular text adheres to or deviates from established conventions

Activity 13.8

Note how these extracts from texts deviate from the expected conventions of the genre.

- What type of text is suggested by the style used?
- After reading the commentary, suggest why the writer has not used the expected conventions of the actual genre.

Extract 1

1 *FIVE MINUTES*

To breathe:

Sit in the lotus position, close your eyes, relax and breathe in deeply.

2 *FIVE MINUTES*

To tone up:

Sit with a straight back, stretch out your arms and bend your body forward as far as you can go.

3 *FIVE MINUTES*

To relax:

Pull your knees up against your chest, put your chin on your knees, then rock forward and backwards and from side to side.

Extract 2

It's pitch black.

You are hundreds of feet underground with millions of tonnes of rock above your head. Suddenly you hear a deep, booming rumble. Something massive is approaching. It sounds like thunder and it's getting closer. You hear shouting and screaming. The air becomes hot, the noise is now deafening. Terrified, you run blindly into the darkness . . .

> **Extract 3**
>
> *Slender white wading birds stalked the still waters of the Kreung Aceh, the river which runs through this devastated city, yesterday. They looked like fastidious little ghosts.*
>
> *It was an oddly tranquil scene for a city which has acquired so many ghosts so quickly, but there was a sense that, if not tranquillity, the beginning of order was stirring among the chaos and destruction.*
>
> *(James Meek, Guardian)*

New genres

The conventions for new genres are emerging through use. In the case of emails, for example, perhaps it is the older generation who need to learn how these differ from letters. The following examples of emails were sent by university students to their tutor.

Activity 13.9

- Note the conventions that the students use in emails to their tutor.
- What opening greetings does each use?
- How do they conclude the message?
- What level of formality is used to convey the assumed relationship?
- Would some seem inappropriate to the recipient?

Email 1

hi alison, saqub here (mmu)

i am a little confused as to what we exactly have to talk about in our 2min presentation on wednesday!

what exactly about the poems do we have to discuss.

p.s when do we get the results back for the assignment?

take care.

Email 2

hi,

sorry to send it so late in the day, please coulkd you let me know if i've reached your required criteria and what i could do to improve my mark, whether the references are correct and what i grade this 1st draft is verging on.

thank you very much

Gershon Walton

Ba, communication, level 1

Email 3

hello!

My name is Joanne Hopkins from your language class on a wed. I am just emailing you for your advice on my essay title. I am thinking about basing it on books for children. Do I have to specify age? What else do I have to include in my title? Eak! I'm stuck!

Thank you!!

From Jo!

Email 4

Hello,

I appreciate that you're very busy at the moment with checking essays, so I've tried to go over it myself. It would be great if you could check it for me as well though.

Thanks,

Matt

Email 5

Dear Alison,

For my essay i have decided to look into reality television and the physocological effects on their audiences/different discourses. This is an area which interests me very much so i would be very gratefull for any feedback you have to enable me to wirte a successfull essay.

With reagards

Sarah Allen

The next chapter explores how language is interpreted in its social context, applying some ideas from pragmatics to the study of spoken language.

14

Pragmatics

This final chapter introduces some concepts from the area of pragmatics to explore the ways that meanings are conveyed between language users. In everyday use, the word 'pragmatic' means 'practical'. The study of pragmatics is also practical, in the sense that it concentrates on the effects of language use in specific social contexts. Although pragmatics is a relatively new area of language study, the ideas are familiar. The question 'What did you mean when you said that?' shows how we are accustomed to 'read between the lines' and work out what is implied.

> **Year 8:** identify the ways implied and explicit meanings are conveyed in different texts, e.g. irony, satire

> **Year 8:** experiment with different language choices to imply meaning and to establish the tone of a piece, e.g. ironic, indignant

> **Year 7:** extend their spoken repertoire by experimenting with language in different roles and dramatic contexts

> **Year 7:** infer and deduce meanings using evidence in the text, identifying where and how meanings are implied

As Chapter 12 showed, it is not enough to understand the literal meaning of words, as they may be used in figurative or emotive ways. Pupils also need to understand the ways that social conventions – particularly of politeness – affect the way we use and interpret language. This chapter concentrates on spoken language. The terms and concepts can be applied to pupils' own speaking skills in discussions and role play of various situations.

Activities highlight aspects of spoken interaction: the formality of the situation, the status, gender, age, social background of the speakers and their relationship. The *manner* in which people speak is shown to be as significant as *what* they say; for example, saying too little or too much, changing the subject, use of taboo language, slang or jargon. Examples demonstrate the significance of phonological features such as stress, intonation, volume and speed in conveying implicit meanings. The potential for misunderstanding between different cultural groups is introduced as a topic for further exploration.

These pragmatic concepts are also useful in analysis of written texts such as drama and dramatic monologues. The first section looks at some important differences between spoken and written language.

Features of spoken language

Written language has been the subject of study for centuries, leaving spoken language relatively ignored. As a result, spoken language has often been seen as a 'poor relation' of written language. Differences in forms and structure tend to be explained using a deficit model, so that features of speech are described as 'sloppy' or 'incorrect'. Recent developments in technology have made recordings and transcripts of spoken language available for systematic research.

The following research findings are taken from the CANCODE project (universities of Cambridge and Nottingham), based on a corpus of five million words of spoken language, alongside a similar corpus of written language (Carter, 2004). The lists in Table 14.1 show the most frequently used words in contemporary speech and writing.

Key words
non-fluency features   interaction   vague language   ellipsis

The top forty words

TABLE 14.1 The top forty words

Spoken language		Written language	
1	the	1	the
2	I	2	to
3	and	3	and
4	you	4	of
5	it	5	a
6	to	6	in
7	a	7	was
8	yeah	8	it
9	that	9	I
10	of	10	he
11	in	11	that
12	was	12	she
13	it's	13	for
14	know	14	on
15	mm	15	her

TABLE 14.1 The top forty words (continued)

Spoken language		Written language	
16	is	16	you
17	er	17	is
18	but	18	with
19	so	19	his
20	they	20	had
21	on	21	as
22	oh	22	at
23	we	23	but
24	have	24	be
25	no	25	have
26	laughs	26	from
27	well	27	not
28	like	28	they
29	what	29	by
30	do	30	this
31	right	31	are
32	just	32	were
33	he	33	all
34	for	34	him
35	erm	35	up
36	be	36	an
37	this	37	said
38	all	38	there
39	there	39	one
40	got	40	been

This statistical evidence highlights some interesting differences between the vocabulary used in spoken (as opposed to written) language. In writing, the most frequently used words are grammatical classes: determiners, pronouns, conjunctions, prepositions and auxiliary verbs. There are only a few content word classes, such as the main verb 'got'. For obvious reasons, the voiced 'fillers' '– mm', 'er', 'erm' – are not common in written language. These **non-fluency features** can be explained by the spontaneous, unplanned nature of spoken language. But there are a number of other words that we use very often when speaking but less frequently in writing.

Can such words be dismissed as simply informal or vague? Carter (2004) suggests that the essential quality of spoken language is that it is interactive, used to keep open a dialogue between speakers. Written language, on the other hand, is essentially a monologue, with little real possibility for **interaction** between writer and reader.

Activity 14.1 asks pupils to reflect on the ways some common words function in spoken language.

Activity 14.1

- Comment on the frequency of these words in spoken language:

    8 yeah

    14 know

    19 so

    27 well

    28 like

    30 do

    31 right

    32 just

- Consider the literal meanings of each word and the ways they function in interaction.

Interaction

The interactive nature of speech is the significant factor in accounting for these differences between the vocabulary of spoken and written language. In written language, the writer must supply all the necessary information, as there is no chance for clarification. The use of **vague language** is a common feature of speech. This negative term suggests that these features are accidental and should be avoided, if possible.

Carter (2004) prefers the term 'deliberately vague' language, to indicate the ways that speakers interact. He suggests that precision is inappropriate in many informal contexts; that some hesitancy keeps the dialogue open. Pupils should be able to adapt their speaking style: what is appropriate between friends in casual conversation may not be effective in more public contexts. But there are some changes in attitudes towards levels of formality in speech.

Even in more formal situations these days, the speaker may use tentative phrases, such as 'sort of' or 'kind of'. One effect is to make the speaker sound more 'human' and approachable. Tony Blair has been compared to Margaret Thatcher for his less assertive style of speaking in many contexts. This choice of style is clearly deliberate – he did not use it over the Iraq war, when a tone of authority was needed. I have also noticed, for example, that some recorded telephone promotional messages use a lot of 'ers' and 'ums' as a way of sounding more friendly, even though they have been deliberately scripted to sell something.

Another striking feature of spoken language is the use of **ellipsis**. This term refers to abbreviated structures, often omitting the subject, such as:

[I]	*Didn't know that film was on tonight.*
[It/That]	*Sounds good to me.*
[There are]	*Lots of things to tell you about the trip to Barcelona.*

This is appropriate in spoken interaction, but should only be used in written language to convey an informal, colloquial voice. The next section introduces some terms from pragmatics to explore the ways meanings are implied in speech.

Implied meanings

Key words

manner   ambiguity   vagueness   omission
roles   relationship   subtext   implied meanings

Language in use

You and I, the characters which grow on a page, most of the time we're inexpressive, giving little away, unreliable, elusive, evasive, obstructive, unwilling. But it's out of these attributes that a language arises. A language ... where, under what is said, another thing is being said.

It is the pause which shows to the audience that the real preoccupation of the characters, the unspoken subtext, is going on beneath the surface, but that it is unable to come into the open. There are two silences: one when no word is spoken; the other when perhaps a torrent of language is employed. Pinter's speech is speaking of a language locked beneath it; that it is continual reference. The speech we hear is an indication of that we don't hear. It is a necessary avoidance, a violent, sly, anguished or mocking smokescreen which keeps the other in its place. When true silence falls we are still left with echo but are nearer nakedness. One way of looking at speech is to say that it is a constant stratagem to cover nakedness (Esslin, 1982).

These comments by the playwright Harold Pinter provide an informal introduction to some concepts in pragmatics. He explains how a character's manner of speaking can convey more than the words actually spoken. Indeed, he suggests that speech is a 'stratagem', used for concealment, rather than direct expression. His characters use language as a 'smokescreen' to avoid giving away their real preoccupations, but they reveal themselves in their pauses and inconsequential speech.

The philosopher H. P. Grice (1975) was also interested in the ways that meanings are implied by the manner of speaking. He suggests that there are four maxims or Co-operative Principles of conversation. This is a simplified outline.

Quantity If someone says rather more/less than we would expect, what do we infer?

Quality If someone says something factually untrue, what did they mean to convey?

Manner If someone communicates in an obscure manner, what do we infer?

Relation If someone changes the subject, what do we infer?

His theory relates to some concepts mentioned in the Framework: pupils should be aware of the meanings implied by **omission**, **ambiguity** and **vagueness**. It is not possible, however, to say that a particular manner of speaking has a fixed effect, or meaning. It depends on the situation – the **roles** of the speakers, their **relationship**, etc. A person who says too little, for example, might convey nervousness, hostility, evasion, dislike ... or it may simply be their personal style.

There are various ways to explore these aspects of implied meanings in spoken language. Interviews with politicians can be studied for the manner in which the interviewee manages awkward questions – often avoiding a clear, brief answer. Pupils

> **Year 7:** extend their spoken repertoire by experimenting with language in different roles and dramatic contexts

can role-play a conversation in pairs, where one has been given the instruction to 'flout' one of the four maxims above. Afterwards, the other should comment on the meanings conveyed by this manner of speaking.

Many drama books suggest activities based on the idea of status – that people adopt roles in interaction, some preferring 'high-status role playing' and others 'low-status role playing'. In the following activity, pupils take turns to choose a playing card, which represents the degree of status they should adopt. They should convey this both by body language and the way they speak.

Activity 14.2

- Take any playing card from a standard 52-card pack.
- Enter the classroom 'late', say something, then take a seat.
- Observers must guess which card is held and explain their reasons.

Application to literary texts

The concept of **subtext** is familiar in literature study to refer to the underlying meanings conveyed to the audience by the scripted dialogue of characters. In pragmatics, the focus is also on **implied meanings**:

> not so much what the *sentence* means, but what the *speaker* means when they utter it

As Pinter comments, there is the 'surface' of what is said, with other things 'going on beneath the surface'. By responding to various clues, language users become skilled in reading between the lines.

Dramatic monologues often exploit this tension between the understanding shared by the author and the audience, and the overt words of the speaker. In the monologues of Alan Bennett, the speakers usually lack self-awareness, but betray themselves through their words. Robert Browning created more devious characters in poetic monologues such as 'My Last Duchess'.

The most extreme gap between the surface and implied meaning occurs with negative statements. As Shakespeare's character Hamlet comments, 'the lady doth protest too much'. Denials tend to imply guilt, particularly if they are elaborate. Some pupils coined the informal term 'mention-itis' for the repeated reference to a particular name. Even if the explicit message is 'I can't stand so-and-so', once a negative thought has been mentioned, the idea makes more impact than the denial. This type of response is illustrated in the next activity.

Activity 14.3

- Read the following extract of dialogue from Shakespeare's *Othello*.
- What is Iago's overt message to Othello?
- What does he imply by these words?

Othello:	*Was that not Cassio parted from my wife?*
Iago:	*Cassio, my lord? No, sure, I cannot think it*
	That he would sneak away so guilty-like,
	Seeing you coming.

Awareness of social conventions

Examples from literature often rely on a shared interpretation – in some ways, a universal response to human psychology – so that vehement denials conventionally imply guilt. But many conventions are specific to a particular social context. This means that language cannot be fully understood by 'outsiders'. This section begins with the ways that misunderstandings can occur in social interaction.

<table>
<tr><td colspan="4">**Key words**</td></tr>
</table>

assumptions	inference	implication	phatic
idioms	politeness	back-channel	

Language in use

Have you got any stamps?
Do you need first or second class?
I didn't say I wished to purchase stamps. I was simply enquiring whether you have any.

Many humorous texts provide useful examples of pragmatic breakdown – such as in the case of a socially inept character who lacks awareness of implied meanings. In the example above, the cartoon character, Mr Logic, in *Viz* magazine, insists on using language in a literal way. He does not appreciate the conventional use of a question – 'Have you got any stamps?' – as a request for goods.

Pupils become skilled in interpreting implied meanings in conversations, asking themselves 'What did he/she mean, when they said that?'

For example, the familiar reproach 'What time do you call this?' is expressed as an interrogative, but a response to the overt question would be regarded as cheeky.

In pragmatics, speech act theory (Austin, 1962; Searle, 1969) offers several useful points about the ways that language conveys meanings. The form of a sentence in isolation can be explained for its explicit sense, but its function in a particular context may be different.

	Form	*Function*
Have you got any stamps?	*interrogative*	*request*
That's right, just leave your clothes all over the floor.	*imperative*	*reproach*

In non-academic jargon, we use terms such as 'loaded questions' and 'weasel words' to indicate that the implied meaning is distinct from the explicit. For example,

Are you telling me that – as a mother who should be concerned to teach her child right from wrong – you colluded in this?
With respect... If my honourable colleague...

The academic terms used are:

- presupposition assumptions – what is already known?
- inference what does the listener infer/guess?
- implicature implications – what is the speaker suggesting/implying?

The area of presupposition – **assumptions** – is specific to a particular social context. The following short conversation illustrates the concept of **assumptions** specific to a social community and shows the **effect** on **implication** and **inference**.

Activity 14.4

- What assumptions are required to interpret the force of Shirley's comment to Alison?
- In what social contexts, might the inference/implication be missed?

(Three women talking over a pot of tea.)

Shirley	*Do you want a biscuit?*
Alison	*Yes, please.*
Charlotte	*No, thanks.*
Shirley	*(to Alison) Charlotte's getting married next month.*

Social expressions

Much spoken language is **phatic** – social pleasantry, with little meaningful content. The conventions differ from one speech community to another. In the UK, for example, 'How are you?' is a friendly greeting, rather than an enquiry about the other's health. This means that misunderstandings often occur between speakers of different backgrounds. An extreme example of this can be found in the popular TV series *Buffy the Vampire Slayer*. Some of the characters are aliens or robots programmed with a complete knowledge of English, but lacking experience of life in the language community. The following extract comments on the way service encounters are concluded in the USA.

Language in use

(Speaking to customer at counter at end of transaction)

Anya	*(smiling) Please go.*
Xander	*Anya, the Shopkeepers Union of America called. They want me to tell you that 'Please go' just got replaced by 'Have a nice day.'*
Anya	*But I have their money. Who cares what sort of day they have?*
Xander	*No one. It's just a long cultural tradition of raging insincerity.*
	(Embrace)
Anya	*(calling out to customer) Hey, you! Have a nice day!*
Xander	*There's my girl.*

(No Place like Home)

Idioms are phrases in a language that cannot be understood by a literal translation. This point is illustrated in a comedy sketch by Alastair MacGowan, where the Swedish football manager Sven Goran Erikkson struggles to understands the idiom 'Tell me about it'. The first time it is used (implying 'I know exactly what you mean') he takes it literally and launches into a detailed explanation. The idiomatic meaning is explained to him, so he remains silent when it is repeated later in the conversation. This time the phrase is used in its literal sense: 'Please elaborate and give me more information.'

The way in which a person speaks affects the meanings conveyed, as much as the content of what they say. Phonological changes in stress, intonation and volume will convey a range of meanings. These may be missed by non-native speakers of English. This can be shown by taking a single word, or short phrase, and using it in different contexts.

> **Year 8:** identify the ways implied and explicit meanings are conveyed in different texts, e.g. irony, satire

---

Activity 14.5

- Devise some short dialogues where one person utters the words 'Thank you'.
- What different meanings can this phrase convey?
- What aspects of phonology – e.g. stress, volume and intonation – affect the implied meanings?

Politeness strategies

As pragmatics is the study of language in use, it emphasises language as a form of social interaction, whereby users negotiate a web of human needs, such as:

- presenting a persona
- trying to be accepted/liked
- being polite/friendly to others
- managing to get what we want.

Although talk may seem spontaneous and straightforward, it requires complex skills to achieve effective interaction. The notion of **politeness** is used in a broad sense to refer to the different types of relationships established in talk. These range from the most informal to the most formal situations.

The social anthropologists Brown and Levinson (1978) use the concept of 'face' needs. They use this term to refer to our public self-image. There are two aspects to this concept:

> ***positive face*** *our need to be liked and accepted*
> ***negative face*** *our right not to be imposed on*

They suggest that speakers use positive politeness strategies with friends to emphasise solidarity, such as:

- shared dialect
- informal lexis
- informal grammar
- more direct requests

Negative politeness strategies, on the other hand, emphasise respect when there is a social distance between speakers, so the following would be used:

- more formal lexis and grammar
- indirect requests.

In this view of politeness, speakers must show an awareness of the others' face needs and vary their manner of speaking according to the situation. Of course, individuals also use these politeness strategies to achieve their own needs. The situation is often quite complex, as speakers adjust the degree of formality in subtle ways.

The sociologist Erving Goffman (1981) uses the term 'footing' to refer to a speaker's stance, or relationship to the other participant. This may change slightly over the course of the conversation, as the need for friendliness is replaced by respect, or vice versa. These shifts in footing are indicated by changes in language use.

Conversations between a boss and employee, parent and child, or teacher and pupil, often reveal subtle changes in footing that pupils will recognise. These are often exaggerated for comic purposes. The following extract is taken from the TV comedy 'mockumentary' *The Office*.

Activity 14.6

- What footing does the manager David Brent adopt towards his receptionist, Dawn?
- How does this change during their conversation?
- What does this reveal about their underlying attitudes to each other?

Brent: *Be gentle with me today, Dawn.*

Dawn: *(EXASPERATED) Yeah? Why's that?*

Brent: *Oh God. Had a skinful last night. I was out with Finchy.*

(TO CAMERA CREW) Chris Finch.

(TO DAWN) Had us on a pub crawl. 'El vino did flow'...

BRENT MIMES DRINKING

Brent: *I was bl...blattered...bl...bladdered...blotto'd...Oh, don't ever come out with me and Finchy.*

Dawn: *No, I won't.*

Brent: *There's guys my age, and they look fifty...How old do you think I look?*

Dawn: *Thirty—*

Brent: *(interrupting) Thirty, yeah...About that. Oh, but I will have to slow down.*

Drinking a bit too much...

BRENT PATS HIS BELLY.

Brent: *...If every single night of the week is too much.*

> **Dawn:** *(joking)... And every lunchtime.*
>
> *BEAT. BRENT TURNS, SUDDENLY A VICIOUS LOOK IN HIS EYES.*
>
> **Brent:** *How many have I had this week?*
>
> **Dawn:** *What?*
>
> **Brent:** *How many pints have I had this week? If you're counting...*
>
> **Dawn:** *I'm not counting.*
>
> **Brent:** *Aren't you? Hmm, you seem to know a lot about my drinking. Does it offend you, eh? You know, getting a little bit... a little bit personal. Imagine if I started doing that with you. I could look at you and come out with something really witty and biting like 'You're a bit...'*
>
> *HE CAN'T THINK OF ANYTHING.*
>
> **Brent:** *...but I don't. Because I'm a professional and professionalism is... and that is what I want, okay? That's all. That's a shame.*
>
> *HE STRIDES OFF, LEAVING DAWN SPEECHLESS.*

Interacting in various situations

Pupils need to be aware of the conventions for various social situations, in particular the needs of more formal conversations. There are many manuals and websites providing advice for successful speaking in business encounters and interviews. Such advice covers various aspects of the manner in which we speak.

Tone of voice	*Speak clearly, don't mumble. Alter pitch to avoid a monotone.*
Standard English	*Choose speaking style aware of non-standard varieties.*
Body language	*Maintain steady eye contact.*

But, equally important is the way we take part as a listener. **Back-channel** behaviour provides vocalised indications of support and encouragement, as the other speaks: 'mm', 'yeah', 'right', etc.

Other advice relates to the 'face needs' of the other:

- Demonstrate that the other person is the centre of attention.
- Use the name of a new acquaintance frequently.
- Wait until you have established credibility before you challenge another's statements.
- Be careful with humour.

This common-sense advice is similar to pragmatic theories. The linguist Robin Lakoff suggests a politeness principle with three maxims:

1 Don't impose.

2 Give options.

3 Be friendly / Make your receiver feel good.

Depending on the situation, one maxim may be emphasised more than the others – the first is similar to negative politeness strategies used in more formal encounters; the third, like positive politeness, tends to occur between friends. However, the style of interaction chosen also varies in different social groups – the British often find Americans 'in your face', and vice versa.

Another linguist, Deborah Tannen, has written several accessible books on spoken interaction – e.g. *You Just Don't Understand* (1990); *That's Not What I Meant* – providing examples of the ways misunderstandings occur if people (often males and females talking to each other) have different styles of interaction.

Another useful concept is suggested by the sociologist Howard Giles. Participants in any interaction often take cues from each other and adapt their manner of speaking. Giles uses the terms 'convergence' and 'divergence' for these changes in style and suggests that:

Convergence happens when an individual adjusts his speech patterns to *match* those of people belonging to another social group. It expresses a feeling of shared identity. **Divergence** happens when an individual adjusts his speech patterns to be *distinct* from those of people belonging to another social group. It expresses a feeling of separation (Giles and Smith, 1979).

In role-play activities, pupils could explore the nature of the interaction using these ideas.

Intonation

This chapter – and the book – ends with some observations on a feature of language variation and change. Tone of voice plays an important part in conveying meanings in English. One simple distinction is between a falling or rising intonation at the end of an utterance. In English, a falling tone signals a definite stance, for statements or instructions. A rising tone signals a question.

Pupils will probably have noticed the contemporary habit of using a rising tone at the end of statements, so that they sound like questions. There are various terms for this: 'HRT' (high-rise terminals) or the informal 'uptalk'.

It is worth considering this feature of language objectively – who uses it, when they use it, what meanings are implied. The final activity asks pupils to comment on this phenomenon of language change and variation. The comments are taken from an accessible article by journalist Matt Seaton on 'uptalk' (*Guardian*, 21 September 2001), which can be accessed from the internet.

Activity 14.7

- Have you noticed 'uptalk' (HRT – a rising intonation at the end of statements)?
- What do you think this way of speaking implies?
- Do you agree, or disagree, with these comments?

The features can be described explicitly: new words, unusual structures, changes in pronunciation, etc. We can ask objective questions: Where did it come from? Who uses it? But, to understand the effect in the widest sense, we need to recognise the subjective responses to language use. In the case of 'uptalk', attitudes to this manner of speaking are generally negative. Perhaps this is true for any new habits introduced by the younger generation, particularly if they originate in the USA? And yet attitudes to language evolve. As pupils need to adapt to the established conventions, so older people may need to catch up with a changing world.

References

Abley, M. (2003) *Spoken Here: Travel Among Threatened Languages*, London: Arrow.

Aitchison, J. (1996) *The Seeds of Speech*, Cambridge: Cambridge University Press.

Austin, J. L. (1962) *How to Do Things with Words*, Cambridge: Harvard University Press.

Bierce, A. (2003) *The Devil's Dictionary*, London: Bloomsbury.

Brown, J. (1971) *Programmed Vocabulary*, Meredith: Prentice-Hall.

Brown, P. and Levinson, S. (1978) *Politeness: Some Universals in Language Usage*, Cambridge: Cambridge University Press.

Carter, R. (2004) *Language and Creativity: The Art of Common Talk*, London: Routledge.

Chomsky, N. (1970) *Language and Mind*, New York: Harcourt Brace Jovanovich.

Crystal, D. (1995) *The Cambridge Encyclopedia of the English Language*, Cambridge: Cambridge University Press.

Crystal, D. (1998) *Language Play*, Harmondsworth: Penguin.

Crystal, D. (2001) *Language and the Internet*, Cambridge: Cambridge University Press.

DfEE/QCA (2000) *The National Curriculum: Handbook for Secondary Teachers in England: Key Stages 3 and 4*, London: HMSO.

DfES (2001) *The Framework for Teaching English: Years 7, 8 and 9*, London: HMSO.

Esslin, M. (1982) *Pinter the Playwright*, London: Methuen.

Fairclough, N. (2000) *New Labour, New Language*, London: Routledge.

Firth, J. R. (1964) *Tongues of Men and Speech*, Oxford: Oxford University Press.

Fowler, H. (1965) *Dictionary of Modern English Usage*, 2nd edition, Oxford: Oxford University Press.

Freire, P. (1970) *Pedagogy of the Oppressed*, New York: Herder and Herder.

Freire, P. (1973) *Education for Critical Consciousness*, New York: Continuum Books.

Giles, H. and Smith, P. (1979) 'Accommodation theory: optimal levels of convergence', in *Language and Social Psychology*, ed. H. Giles and R. N. St Clair, Baltimore, MD: University Park Press.

Goddard, A. (1996) 'Tall stories: the metaphorical nature of everyday talk', *English Education* 30(2), National Association for the Teaching of English.

Goffman, E. (1981) *Forms of Talk*, Oxford: Oxford University Press.

Grice, H. P. (1975) 'Logic and conversation', in *Syntax and Semantics*, vol. 3, *Speech Acts*, ed. P. Cole and J. Morgan, New York: Academic Press.

Hathorn, L. and Rogers, G. (1994) *Way Home*, London: Andersen Press.

Hodges, R. (1982) *Improving Spelling and Vocabulary in the Secondary School*, ERIC Clearinghouse on Reading and Communication Skills and National Council of Teachers of English.

Holmes, J. (1992) *An Introduction to Sociolinguistics*, London: Longman.

Hudson, R. (1980) *Sociolinguistics*, Cambridge: Cambridge University Press.

Kohler, W. (1947) *Gestalt Psychology*, New York: Liveright.

Lakoff, R. (1975) *Language and Women's Place*, New York: Harper and Row.

McWhorter, J. (1998) *The Word on the Street*, New York: Perseus Books.

National Literacy Strategy (2004) 'Review of research', www.standards.dfes.gov.uk/literacy/publications/research

Peccei, J. (1994) *Child Language*, London: Routledge.

Perfors, A. (2004) 'What's in a name? The effect of sound symbolism on perception of facial attractiveness', poster presented at CogSci, Chicago.

Pinker, S. (1994) *The Language Instinct*, London: HarperCollins.

Raleigh, W. (1926) *On Writers and Writing*, selected and ed. George Gordon, London: Kessinger.

Rosen, M. (2002) *emagazine* (February), London: English and Media Centre.

Sapir, E. (1970) *Language: An Introduction to the Study of Speech*, London: Hart-Davies. First published 1929.

Searle, J. (1969) *Speech Acts: An Essay in the Philosophy of Language*, Cambridge: Cambridge University Press.

Tannen, D. (1990) *You Just Don't Understand: Women and Men in Conversation*, London: Virago Press.

Tomlinson, D. (1994) 'Errors in the research into the effectiveness of grammar teaching', *English in Education* 28: 2–26.

Truss, L. (2003) *Eats, Shoots and Leaves*, London: Profile Books.

Wales, K. (2001) *Dictionary of Stylistics*, Harlow: Longman.

Weekley, E. (1929) *The English Language*, London: André Deutsch.

Wilkinson, A. (1971) *The Foundations of Language: Talking and Reading in Young Children*, Oxford: Oxford University Press.

Index